MANDELA'S DILEMMA

SOUL DIA

Ordering Information:

Prime Seven Media
518 Landmann St.
Tomah City, WI 54660

Printed in the United States of America

Index

"I never lose. I either win or learn."

— Nelson Mandela

Hey there, Adventurer!

Welcome to a wild ride packed with twists, turns, and everything in between! You're about to dive into a world I crafted with the kind of fervor that keeps me up at night, heart racing like a jackrabbit. How did this book come to life, you ask? Well, grab your favorite snack—maybe popcorn or even some funky chips—because I'm about to unfold a tale that led to its creation.

It all started one starlit night, the kind where inspiration crashes into you like a runaway train. I found myself wrestling with thoughts and ideas that had been bubbling up for years, and suddenly, lightning struck! The vision for this book took shape right before my eyes. Nights turned into mornings as I sketched out characters, settings, and wild adventures. You wouldn't believe how the creative process unfolded, it was like a rollercoaster ride—thrilling, anxiety-inducing, and exhilarating all at once!

Research? Oh, let me tell you about that! I went down rabbit holes like a curious Alice, exploring everything from ancient myths to modern-day conspiracies. I took notes, scribbled in margins, and even whispered sweet nothings to my laptop. There's an energy that comes from hunting down facts and stories that just gets my blood pumping! It's like being a treasure hunter, digging through the sands of time to uncover hidden gems that could sparkle in the reader's imagination.

As I shaped the narrative, I poured my heart and soul into crafting characters that would leap off the pages, characters full of quirks and charm that you can't help but cheer for (or sometimes against). Their struggles, triumphs, and epic fails are all wrapped in a journey you won't soon forget! The development of this book was like assembling a dazzling puzzle where each piece plays a crucial role in the bigger picture.

I want you to feel the exhilaration that I felt when I crafted each chapter. Every twist and turn holds a nugget of wisdom or a laugh-out-loud moment waiting just for you. So, buckle up! Because as you plunge into these pages, be ready to embark on an unforgettable adventure.

I remind you, dear reader, that this isn't just my story—it's ours. Your thoughts will dance with my words, creating a magnificent tapestry woven from shared dreams and experiences. It's like passing a baton in a relay race, and I can't wait for you to take it and run!

So, what do you say? Are you ready to turn the page and leap into this whirlwind of excitement? There will be ups, there will be downs, and every moment of it will be electric. The world I built is waiting—not just for my words to shine but for YOU to engage and become part of this narrative.

Let's dive right in! I promise you, by the time you turn the last page, you'll be buzzing with inspiration, teetering on the edge of what to explore next. Each chapter is a door opening to new revelations. So, keep that explorer spirit alive and set your curiosity ablaze!

Truly, I couldn't be more thrilled for you to read this book. Each word is laced with excitement and intention, crafted to ensure you don't just read, but rather experience every ounce of its energy. Let's venture together through realms of imagination and possibility, forever changing the way you view the world. Get ready, friend, because the adventure is about to begin!

Forever excited to have you here,

With all my fervor,

SOUL DIA

The Spark of
Activism

*"There is no passion to be found playing
small — in settling for a life that is less
than the one you are capable of living."*

— Nelson Mandela

Origins of a Revolutionary Spirit

Nelson Rolihlahla Mandela was born on July 18, 1918, in the small rural village of Mvezo, a place nestled deep in the heart of the Eastern Cape of South Africa. This environment, steeped in the traditions of the Xhosa people, would profoundly shape his identity and the revolutionary spirit that he would come to embody. Understanding Mandela's early years requires a close examination of both the familial and cultural influences that surrounded him, as well as the systemic injustices that he would later dedicate his life to fighting against.

Mandela was born into the Madiba clan, a lineage that held significant cultural weight among the Xhosa. His father, Gadla Henry Mphakanyiswa, served as a chief, a position of respect and authority within the tribal community. The values of leadership, service, and responsibility were ingrained in Mandela from a young age through both familial expectations and the cultures embedded in Xhosa tribal life. He was raised with the understanding that one's duty was not only to oneself but to the community at large—a theme that would resonate through his life and political beliefs.

> **"I have cherished the ideal of a democratic and free society in which all persons live together in harmony and with equal opportunities."**
>
> — Nelson Mandela

As a child, Mandela was known as "Rolihlahla," a name that means "pulling the branch of a tree" or, more pointedly, "troublemaker." This moniker would later carry a certain irony, as Mandela would indeed become a significant "troublemaker" for the apartheid regime in South Africa. His early life in Mvezo was marked with simplicity, but it was also filled with vibrant cultural practices. The Xhosa were known for their rich oral traditions, storytelling, music, and ceremonies that celebrated milestones and highlighted the value of the community. Although life was often harsh, the sense of belonging and cultural cohesion within the village provided Mandela a secure platform from which he could explore the world beyond.

At the age of seven, Mandela was sent to a local mission school where he would encounter not only the joys of education but also the stark realities of racial injustice for the first time. In this school, he received both Western and African education, the latter serving as a crucial foundation for his identity. More importantly, it was here that he began to grasp the complexities of apartheid—a practice designed to oppress and segregate the black majority from the white minority in South Africa.

In his formative years, Mandela's teachers played a significant role in shaping his views. One teacher, a missionary named Mr. J. P. N. C. G. de Villiers, encouraged him to read about the history of the African continent, introducing him to prominent figures from across Africa. Through these stories, Mandela's understanding of oppression deepened, and his desire for justice began to take root. He learned about the rich histories of African kingdoms, the struggles against colonialism, and the ongoing fight for equality. These lessons became pivotal in forming his growing sense of justice and resistance.

Mandela's awareness of his own racial identity crystallized during an incident that would remain etched in his memory. One day, he was playing with his white friend, and when the boy's father learned of their friendship, he forbade his son from associating with him because of Mandela's background. This pivotal moment exposed a painful truth: the dictates of apartheid would not allow genuine friendships to flourish between races. This revelation about the limitations imposed on him—and on black South Africans more broadly—ignited a sense of injustice in him that would continue to simmer throughout his youth.

The teachings of his mentor, as well as the pain of social divisions he witnessed, encouraged Mandela to seek answers. He participated in school debates and began to express his views more openly. His desire for knowledge was relentless, and with it came an ever-growing ambition to challenge the societal status quo. In private conversations, he would speak passionately about the aspirations of his people, unable to reconcile the dreams of freedom and equality he envisioned with the harsh realities of racial segregation.

Community was central to Mandela's upbringing. The Xhosa tradition emphasized collective action and the interconnectedness of community life. He often took part in communal activities, where elders would share wisdom from the past, recount battles fought for freedom, and discuss strategies for the future. These gatherings instilled in him a profound sense of purpose and duty—a feeling that any progress would be achieved through collective struggle rather than individual ambition.

His defiance against the status quo was further fueled by his admiration for key figures in African history, such as Shaka Zulu and other tribal leaders. These figures represented a legacy of struggle and triumph that ignited a revolutionary flame within him. He learned of the resistance against colonial powers, and the ethos of fighting for dignity and respect became ingrained in his psyche. History was not merely a series of events; it became a beckoning call to action that would later define his own journey.

When Mandela moved from Mvezo to the larger township of Qunu, he encountered a more diverse and complex social fabric. The presence of various ethnic groups introduced him to a broader spectrum of injustices. The idea of unity among disparate voices— each bearing unique stories of suffering and resilience—became an enduring theme in his life's work.

As a teenager, Mandela joined a local school, where he faced new challenges, including increased exposure to colonial ideologies and practices. This transition was marked by moments of rebelliousness, as he began to question not only the realities of apartheid but also the methods of resistance employed by previous generations. He immersed himself in literature, devouring books that exposed him to revolutionary thought from across the globe, including such pivotal texts as Marx's "The Communist Manifesto" and writings from leaders such as Mahatma Gandhi.

In high school, he struggled to balance his aspirations for education with the economic hardships faced by his family. Yet, through perseverance and determination, Mandela succeeded in completing his studies. His own ambitions led him to continue his education at the University of Fort Hare, an institution meant for black South Africans, where he was confronted by systemic issues even more directly tied to apartheid.

At Fort Hare, Mandela was initiated into a political environment that would sharpen his revolutionary spirit. He engaged in debates and formed friendships with like-minded individuals who shared a common goal of dismantling the apartheid regime. This was a period marked by awakening and organization, as students began advocating for their rights and challenging oppressive policies. During this time, Mandela thirsted for justice and began to understand the importance of organized resistance.

Mandela's actions during his university years laid the groundwork for his participation in the African National Congress. The expertly crafted campaigns initiated by older leaders inspired him to step out of his comfort zone and become directly involved in the struggle. He organized protests and mobilized students, tapping into the fervor that swept through young activists yearning for change.

These intimate experiences fostered in Mandela a profound understanding of unity—he learned that individuals are powerless alone, but together they can forge an unstoppable force for justice. His humility before the elders, coupled with his own passionate vision for a free South Africa, became the scaffolding around which his activism would build.

In the aftermath of his studies, Mandela's journey would take him from the confines of academia to the gritty streets of activism. Armed with a sense of purpose and community, he began actively engaging with multinational efforts to ignite change, recognizing that the liberation of his people was intrinsically tied to a broader struggle for human rights and equality.

By exploring Mandela's childhood and formative experiences in Mvezo and Qunu, we begin to see the roots of a revolutionary spirit that would defy colonialism and apartheid. The early influences from his family, his cultural heritage, and his community sparked a passion that would not be extinguished despite all odds. Through pivotal moments of realization against racial injustices and the inspirational figures in history that fueled his awakening, Mandela's journey as a leader began to unfold.

Ultimately, it was in these early years, amidst the rich tapestry of Xhosa culture and entrenched inequities, that Nelson Mandela's resolve was forged. The bonds he formed with communal traditions and the aspirations of his people propelled him towards a destiny that would not only redefine his life but would also reshape the future of an entire nation.

Inspiration from Struggle

Nelson Mandela's early foray into activism was fundamentally shaped by the figures and events that resonated deeply within the broader struggle for justice and equality, not only within South Africa but across the globe. These influences would steer him on a path towards leadership, culminating in his pivotal role in the anti-apartheid movement. From his formative years in the rural village of Mvezo to the bustling urban landscape of Johannesburg, the inspiration he drew from both local traditions and international movements was integral in crystallizing his understanding of activism.

Mandela grew up during a time when the harsh realities of racial discrimination were becoming increasingly apparent. His early encounters with injustice—such as the limitations placed on black people's access to education and opportunities—sharpened his awareness of the inequities embedded in the fabric of South African society. But it was not merely personal experiences that forged his political outlook; it was the considerable influence of key figures and significant historical events that ignited the fervor for justice that would define his life.

At the core of Mandela's awakening was the legacy of African leaders who had fought against colonialism and oppression. Figures like Jomo Kenyatta in Kenya, Kwame Nkrumah in Ghana, and Julius Nyerere in Tanzania served as beacons of hope, demonstrating the power of unity and resistance. Their struggles were not only fought on the African continent but also inspired leaders across the globe who were fighting similar battles against imperialism and racial subjugation. As Mandela engaged with these narratives, he found himself invigorated by their commitment to national sovereignty and social justice.

> **"Courage is not the absence of fear — it's inspiring others to move beyond it."**
>
> — Nelson Mandela

The seeds of Mandela's activism were further nurtured by the global movements arising in the wake of World War II. The establishment of the United Nations and the subsequent adoption of the Universal Declaration of Human Rights in 1948 ignited a widespread awareness of human rights as a universal condition. Activists from various backgrounds—whether in India, the United States, or Latin America—were spearheading movements that challenged colonial rule, advocating for equality, and promoting self-determination. It was in this crucible of global consciousness that Mandela began to envision a South Africa free from apartheid's shackles.

Throughout his formative years in Johannesburg, Mandela met individuals whose ideologies would leave an indelible mark on his journey towards activism. The African National Congress (ANC) played a pivotal role in introducing him to like-minded figures who shared his yearning for freedom. Among them was Walter Sisulu, a senior member of the ANC, whose mentorship provided Mandela not only with political knowledge but also critical insight into the structure and history of the organization. Sisulu's emphasis on collective action and community organization inspired Mandela to focus on grassroots mobilization, further entrenching his belief in the power of the people.

In 1944, a significant evolution took place within the ANC with the formation of the African National Congress Youth League. Mandela, alongside a cadre of passionate youth, was instrumental in contending that political mass action and civil disobedience were not merely options but necessities in the struggle against oppression. This shift from passive resistance to a more active approach echoed the rhetoric and tactics of anti-colonial struggles elsewhere against regimes that sought to silence dissent. The axiom of engaging directly with power dynamics became a hallmark of Mandela's strategy.

Moreover, the realities of World War II infused a sense of urgency into global discussions on tyranny and oppression. For

Mandela, the post-war world represented not only the potential for decolonization but also the dangers of lingering imperialist influences. Movements aimed at dismantling colonial rule in Asia and Africa inspired Mandela to adopt a broader perspective of liberation. He recognized that the fight for freedom was not segregated to South Africa—it transcended borders and echoed through every instance of subjugation. This realization crystallized his understanding of activism as both a local and global fight, uniting various strands of resistance into a cohesive narrative.

As Mandela expanded his worldview, encounters with international figures further fueled his enthusiasm for justice. One such encounter was with the American civil rights leader Paul Robeson, whose dedication to racial equality and social justice resonated deeply with Mandela. Robeson's concerts and speeches advocating for justice became a form of resistance against social norms predicated on an oppressive system. During a visit to South Africa in the late 1940s, Robeson addressed apartheid's injustices head-on, reminding Africans, particularly the youth, of their power to create change.

Another pivotal moment occurred during Mandela's time in the African National Congress when he had the opportunity to hear from leading international figures such as the Indian independence leader Mahatma Gandhi, who had pioneered nonviolent resistance. Gandhi's strategies of nonviolent protest reinforced the importance of civil disobedience as a tool for challenging the status quo and creating meaningful change. Mandela began to appreciate how these tactics could apply not only to India's struggle against British colonial rule but also to South Africa's plight under apartheid.

Mandela's encounters with global movements against oppression were not confined to fellow leaders; his interactions with ordinary citizens committed to change also profoundly influenced him. While studying in London during the late 1950s, Mandela was inspired by the British anti-apartheid movement, which showcased solidarity with South African comrades. Activists like Ruth First and the founding members of the Campaign Against Apartheid impressed upon him the power of international advocacy, urging him to harness the wellspring of global solidarity in his fight for justice in South Africa.

The undercurrents of inspiration stemming from diverse activism allowed Mandela to refine his vision for a free South Africa. He recognized that liberation would not merely be the absence of apartheid; it would necessitate an active and inclusive approach toward nation-building after the struggles had concluded. Therefore, the values derived from the civil rights movement, anti-colonialism, and global activism coalesced into a unique understanding of what a free society should embody. This vision included not just the dismantling of oppressive structures but the establishment of social equity, economic justice, and national consciousness among South Africans.

Yet, despite these inspirations, Mandela faced internal and external challenges that tested his growing commitment to activism. The realities of the ANC's ideology regarding racial justice and equality were often hotly debated. As a leader of the ANC Youth League, Mandela was acutely aware of the tension between older and younger generations within the movement. The veterans of the ANC often advocated for patience and negotiation, while the youth, emboldened by global movements, were increasingly inclined toward more assertive measures, including armed resistance.

This discord was exemplified by Mandela's own evolving approach to activism. Initially, he espoused nonviolence, employing tactics of civil disobedience and mobilization as preached by

Gandhian philosophy. However, as the apartheid regime's brutality intensified, Mandela's perspective shifted. Inspired by revolutionary figures abroad, including Fidel Castro and Che Guevara, he began to entertain the notion that armed struggle could serve as a legitimate response when peaceful means failed. The radicalization of his approach did not come easily and created divisions not only within the ANC but also within the broader anti-apartheid movement.

Mandela's jump into armed resistance came with the establishment of Umkhonto we Sizwe (MK)—the military wing of the ANC. This pivotal decision became a hallmark moment in his evolution as a revolutionary leader, reflecting his commitment to pursuing all avenues for liberation. As he prepared for this new trajectory in the early 1960s, Mandela was mindful of the monumental influences from the past: those who had stood against oppression, who had inspired him, and who had crystallized his belief that active resistance was non-negotiable.

As Mandela's journey unfolded, he frequently reflected on the role of inspiration in the construction of revolutionary identities. The figures he admired and encountered served not only as mentors and guides but also set standards for justice and equality that transfused his activism with ambition and authenticity. Each story, each struggle, came together to weave a tapestry of resilience that remained central to Mandela's philosophy.

In the years that followed, Mandela would draw on these varied influences as he emerged as a symbol of resistance, both in prison and beyond. His letters, speeches, and interactions would highlight the importance of these inspirations, conveying his understanding of activism as a collective endeavor—one that transcended individual experiences and was enriched by global dialogues about freedom, equity, and justice.

Ultimately, the influences that ignited Mandela's fervor for justice were multifaceted and deeply interwoven. They formed the backbone of his activism and set the stage for his enduring legacy, which continues to resonate. Inspired by the struggles of great leaders, local communities, and the universal quest for dignity and rights, Mandela became an exemplar of how a conscious engagement with history could inform and ignite a revolutionary spirit. His journey from the rural heart of Mvezo to the corridors of political power was marked by moments of conversion and guidance, fueled by voices that dared to imagine a free South Africa. As Mandela walked this path, he not only navigated his own fires of conviction but also became a lighthouse for future generations inspired to combat injustice and envision a just world.

> **"A good head and a good heart are always a formidable combination."**
>
> — Nelson Mandela

The Birth of the ANC Youth League

In the early 1940s, South Africa was at a critical juncture, with apartheid policies increasingly solidifying, suffocating the aspirations of millions of black South Africans. The oppressive political environment called for a response that could surely rally the nation's youth towards purposeful action. It was during this time, motivated by an acute awareness of injustice and a fervent desire for change, that the African National Congress Youth League (ANCYL) emerged as a formidable entity within the broader anti-apartheid movement. This subchapter aims to dissect the establishment of the Youth League, Nelson Mandela's pivotal role within its inception, the strategies that Youth League leaders employed to galvanize support and infuse militancy into the ANC's vision, and the prevailing tensions that characterized the dynamic between traditional leadership and the radical ideas of the younger generation.

The roots of the ANC Youth League can be traced back to the socio-political landscape of South Africa during the late 1930s. It was an era where the existing African National Congress, historically perceived as a conservative body representing the interests of urban black elites, struggled to resonate with the broader disenfranchised black populace. Many young activists felt a burgeoning sense of frustration with the ANC's approach, which appeared overly conciliatory towards the oppressive government. Studies reveal that frustration among the youth burgeoned into a fierce desire for a more assertive response, one that aligned with the aspirations of a new generation demanding freedom and dignity.

Mandela himself, at the time a young lawyer in Johannesburg, was introduced to the ANC's internal dynamics when he became a member in 1943. Joining in a period marked by economic hardship, racial discrimination, and stagnant governance, he was significantly influenced by the failures of the ANC to mobilize effectively against the government. This dissatisfaction fueled his determination to advocate for a re-imagined political strategy—a movement to bridge traditional goals with the urgent needs of the youth. Mandela, alongside contemporaries like Walter Sisulu and Anton Lembede, was soon witnessing the seeds of a transformative political philosophy that would eventually crystallize into the founding principles of the ANC Youth League.

In April 1944, the ANC Youth League was formally established. The birthplace was the bustling capital of Johannesburg, a city pulsing with life yet suffocated by racial divides. In a stark contrast to the existing ANC leadership, the Youth League heralded a radical approach to activism. The ideology championed by its founders emphasized self-determination, emphasizing that black South Africans possessed the capability to lead their own struggle for rights and justice. They rejected the idea of seeking permission or favor from the ruling authorities, insisting instead on asserting their presence within the political landscape.

One of the primary ambitions of the Youth League was to redefine the nature of the ANC itself. The founders, including Mandela, fervently believed that the ANC must shift from its conservative roots to embody a more proactive stance. The Young Lions, as they were often called, sought to infuse the organization with militance and youth-led initiatives. The result was a revitalized organization with a focus on mass mobilization—a move that would set the stage for a broader resistance against the apartheid regime.

The strategies employed by the Youth League leaders were diverse and deeply impactful. Central to their approach was community engagement and mass mobilization. They recognized the necessity of accessing the collective strength of the South African black populace. This meant establishing grassroots organizations that encouraged local involvement and support. The Youth League organized a myriad of events ranging from lectures and rallies to cultural showcases, including music and poetry that resonated deeply with the people's narratives of struggle.

One notable initiative was the launch of the 'Youth Day'—an event that highlighted the pivotal role of the young in the liberation struggle. The mobilization called upon the youth to embrace their capabilities as agents of transformation. The celebration became a cornerstone of the Youth League's identity, embodying the spirit of resilience and fierce pride that characterized their ethos. Such events instilled a sense of belonging among youth while emphasizing their role as future leaders.

Furthermore, the Youth League aimed to challenge the intellectual limitations imposed by traditional leadership. They were intent on incorporating radical ideas that stemmed from global movements against oppression, drawing inspiration from anti-colonialist struggles in Africa and civil rights movements emerging in the United States. By shifting the narrative to a more revolutionary framework, they forged a new identity that resonated with the aspirations of their contemporaries. This infusion of militance sought to elevate discussions around freedom, justice, and equality.

However, the emergence of the Youth League was not without its challenges. Tensions between the traditional ANC leaders and the radical youth escalated as the older generation clung to diplomatic avenues while the Youth League demanded a bolder stance. The conservatism of existing leaders, many of whom believed in negotiating and engaging with the apartheid government, clashed with the revolutionary ideals that the Youth League fervently championed.

The Younger generation found themselves at a crossroads. The discontent with the ANC's older guard was palpable; many felt that the leadership was out of touch with the realities facing everyday South Africans. Their commitment to a more authoritarian government was perceived as a betrayal of the foundational anti-apartheid aspirations. A historic rift emerged, where Mandela and other Youth League leaders began to articulate their criticisms openly, challenging the ANC's existing frameworks.

One poignant moment that crystallized this generational conflict arose during discussions of the ANC's response to the 1948 election results, when the National Party solidified apartheid into law. Mandela galvanized support within the Youth League, calling for stronger opposition measures which culminated in the introduction of the 1949 Programme of Action. This revolutionary document outlined a plan for widespread mobilization against the oppressive regime, emphasizing boycotts, strikes, and civil disobedience.

The Programme acted as a resonance chamber reflecting the sentiments of radical youth across South Africa. The Youth League leaders dictated new tactics for the struggle: direct action became a significant component of their philosophy. They sought to disrupt the normalized structures of racial oppression, to make crushing apartheid economically viable through sustained collective action.

Despite the mounting internal conflict, the ANC Youth League's influence began to seep into the broader national consciousness. With Mandela and his associates at the helm, the Youth League saw an influx of support and a diverse range of members crossing racial and class lines. In schools, universities, and local communities, the message of resistance began to solidify, inspiring a generation previously marginalized by despair. The Youth League thus established itself as an essential actor in the larger political landscape, marking a departure from simply enduring oppression to actively contesting it.

Furthermore, the ideological underpinnings of the ANC Youth League paved the way for future transformations within the ANC itself. The infusion of militance established a new template for engagement, significantly influencing subsequent actions undertaken by the ANC in the years that followed. The League's radical vision invigorated younger members within the ANC, and with Mandela increasingly assuming leadership roles, the urgency for comprehensive change only intensified.

The dichotomy inherent in the tension between radical youth and traditional ANC leadership continued to manifest throughout this evolving struggle. As the youth argued for immediate and revolutionary changes, the older generation, although gradually acknowledging the essential role youth played within the organization, remained wary of fully endorsing aggressive tactics. Out of this friction would grow a rich tapestry of strategies and ideologies intertwined within the ANC's path towards overthrowing apartheid.

With Mandela's ascendance within the ANC Youth League as a key figure, the organization found itself evolving rapidly. His ability to fuse loyalty to ANC principles with the revolutionary ideas embraced by youth ensured that the League had the tools needed to challenge the traditional party structure. He skillfully navigated between both factions, arguing for a united front that would effectively challenge apartheid while remaining rooted in the broader political spectrum.

> **"During my lifetime I have dedicated myself to this struggle. It is an ideal for which I am prepared to die."**
>
> — Nelson Mandela

Mandela's trajectory in the Youth League exemplified the struggles emblematic of this period. His capacity to advocate for radical change, harnessed with pragmatism, ultimately equipped him with what would become a hallmark of his leadership philosophy. In the nascent years of the Youth League, Mandela's engagement with policy and action reflected a profoundly personal commitment to harnessing the fervor for change coursing through his contemporary generation.

The establishment of the ANC Youth League set the stage for a transformation within the larger liberation movement, catalyzing a new commitment to activism among the youth that would challenge established norms of power. The dialogue championed by Mandela and his compatriots encouraged a movement that spanned generations—one rich in radical ideas framed through the collective experiences of South Africa's people.

Mandela's influence in the Youth League reinforced the notion that for meaningful political change to occur, the involvement of young, passionate activists was not merely beneficial but essential. This understanding laid the groundwork for initiatives that sought to involve and empower the youth in every aspect of the liberation struggle, extending far beyond immediate political objectives. With the establishment of the ANC Youth League, Mandela and his generation symbolized the arrival of a new era of activism that would not just participate in the struggle, but forge the future of an entire nation.

In retrospect, the birth of the ANC Youth League marked a profound moment of awakening in South Africa's political landscape. The organization's formation, propelled by Mandela and his contemporaries, actively infused the spirit of resistance within the collective consciousness of African youth, leading to a seismic cultural shift crucial for the eventual dismantling of apartheid. The tensions and intricacies of this early formative period in the ANC's history serve as both a lesson in political maneuvering and an inspiration for future generations, illustrating the potency of youth engagement when combined with an unwavering commitment to justice.

Chains and Courage

*"I have walked that long road to freedom.
I have tried not to falter; I have made missteps
along the way. But I have discovered the secret
that after climbing a great hill, one only finds
that there are many more hills to climb."*

– Nelson Mandela

Life on Robben Island

Robben Island, a barren landmass just off the coast of Cape Town, was to become the crucible in which Nelson Mandela's political visions and personal resilience were tested over a span of 27 years. The island, known for its harsh and austere conditions, loomed ominously, a remnant of the apartheid government's harsh suppression of dissent. As the boats ferrying prisoners approached, they would often feel the cold winds that swept across the rocky shores, a fitting precursor to the shivers of confinement that awaited within the prison walls.

"Education is the most powerful weapon which you can use to change the world."

— Nelson Mandela

Upon his arrival in 1964, Mandela was stripped of his past, his freedoms, and even his name, reduced to the inmate number 46664. The prison was meticulously designed to dehumanize, with its spartan cells measuring just 2.4 meters by 2.1 meters. These tiny spaces, barely large enough to house a bed and a bucket, lacked basic comforts. The walls were bare, providing no solace or means of distraction from the solitude of imprisonment. Outfitted with only a small mattress, a blanket that offered little warmth, and a table, Mandela and his fellow inmates faced an unyielding environment that tested the very limits of their endurance.

Mandela's daily life on Robben Island was dominated by a rigid schedule orchestrated by the guards, whose treatment mirrored the relentless conditions of the prison itself. Mornings began with a loud clanging of metal, rousing the prisoners from their restless sleep. Breakfast was a meager affair: dry bread and thin porridge that often lacked nutritional value. There was little time to savor these paltry meals as the prisoners were quickly marshaled out for hard labor.

The labor itself was grueling. Men groped in the harsh sunlight, breaking stones into gravel—a task both physically demanding and symbolically oppressive. The work was intended not only to punish but to humiliate, forcing Mandela and his comrades to toil under the watchful eyes of contemptuous guards, their jeering remarks often punctuating the air. Injuries from the sharp stones and the relentless sun served as constant reminders of their plight. But amidst these tribulations, Mandela sought to extract meaning and purpose from the labor, viewing it as an act of resistance rather than subjugation.

The guards, products of a bitterly divided society, often displayed a cruel indifference toward the suffering of the prisoners. The threat of brutality loomed large; whippings and beatings were not uncommon for those who dared to speak up or resist. The psychological torment was equally damaging; the conditions were designed to erode their spirit, stripping them of their identities and reducing them to mere numbers. Mandela was frequently reminded of his status as a prisoner, subjected to a humiliating routine that included degrading searches and control over even the most basic freedoms.

Yet, within this structure of oppression, Mandela displayed a remarkable reservoir of mental fortitude. His spirit resolutely fought against the despair, churning through the suffocation of confinement. While each day blurred into the next, he meticulously crafted an internal life that fortified his resolve. This mental resilience became a key strategy for survival, allowing him to withstand the overwhelming sense of isolation that permeated Robben Island.

In the bleakness of his cell, Mandela found solace in his thoughts and memories, often recalling the spirit of his fellow comrades on the outside. The longing for freedom was never far from his mind. He realized that while the physical walls of the prison encased him, they could not imprison his ideas. He often engaged in deep reflections about strategy and philosophy, which he would later articulate upon his release. Decisions made in isolation took on a potency that underlined his commitment to the ANC's cause, as he imagined the South Africa he yearned to see.

Building alliances and fostering camaraderie among inmates became a critical aspect of Mandela's incarceration. The shared suffering on Robben Island forged an unbreakable bond among the men. They displayed a will to resist the dehumanization tactics of their captors together, often gathering in small groups, reminiscing, and discussing their plans for liberation. The prison became a microcosm of the ANC's broader struggle against apartheid—a space where ideologies were debated, and strategies formulated, despite the barriers of confinement.

In the shadowy corridors of Robben Island, Mandela emerged as a natural leader. He organized discussions that encompassed political education, stressing the importance of maintaining a united front against their oppressors. He emphasized the ideological underpinnings of their struggle, instilling a sense of purpose within the confined walls. Prisoners, regardless of their past rivalries or factions, gathered to discuss politics, history, and culture, creating a vibrant tapestry of intellectual resilience that countered the drudgery of prison life.

Mandela's charisma sparked hope among those that surrounded him. Tales of struggle, bravery, and the shared commitment to fight for a better future echoed through the stone walls, pushing aside the despair that threatened to engulf them. They realized that the prison system was an extension of apartheid's cruelty and that solidarity would become their anchor. The tucked-away corners of the prison were filled with whispered conversations about hope and freedom, punctuated by laughter amid the sorrow, reminding each other of the laughter that awaited them beyond the prison gates.

By cultivating these relationships, Mandela ensured that they would not only survive physically but also academically and emotionally. Education became a secret weapon against the prison's intent to silence them. The prisoners risked severe punishment by continuing their studies, sharing books and notes covertly. They became each other's teachers, unlocking doors to the universe of ideas and thoughts that apartheid sought to seal off forever. Literature by figures like Marx, Lenin, and other revolutionary thinkers permeated their discussions, framing their understanding of their fight as a global struggle in the context of oppressive regimes everywhere.

However, in such an oppressive environment, the specter of hopelessness continuously attempted to infiltrate their defiance. Limited access to the outside world deepened their isolation. The entire country was essentially an antagonistic backdrop, yet the world outside teetered on the brink of change. As news of anti-apartheid demonstrations managed to trickle through the prison walls, Mandela and his comrades absorbed these narratives with undying hope. Each piece of information became a lifeblood, rejuvenating their minds with the possibility that their struggle was not in vain.

As Mandela navigated the challenges of life on Robben Island, he also had to confront the despair that occasionally seeped into his psyche. There were days when the weight of confinement felt particularly suffocating, moments when he teetered on the brink of despair. During these periods, he often turned to visualization, picturing the smiles of his family and the vibrant landscapes of his homeland. He clung to memories of his youth, the sounds of laughter in the streets of Mvezo, and communal celebrations featuring the rich traditions of the Xhosa people. These reminiscences became his refuge, providing moments of escape from the harsh reality surrounding him.

Mental exercises, such as deep reflection and envisioning a free future, played crucial roles in sustaining hope. The struggles faced were acknowledged, but the determination to persevere never wavered. Mandela learned to accept that the path before him would involve sacrifice and struggle. The insights he gained during these moments of contemplation would later inform his political strategies and goals, aligning them with the underlying principles of the ANC and the ideals of freedom that drove him forward.

One of the defining features of life on Robben Island was the inhuman treatment endured at the hands of the authority figures. Guards wielded their power like a weapon, often using both psychological and physical tactics to instill fear. The prisoners were frequently subjected to threats, taunts, and abuse, and Mandela vividly recounted instances where guards would deliberately flout regulations to remind the inmates of their power. Yet, Mandela maintained that even in the face of such oppression, they could not let their spirits be extinguished. His framework of hope inspired a courage within the prisoners, transcending the immediate brutality inflicted upon them.

With time, instances of defiance began to bloom from the cracks in the stone walls. Sowing resistance became a means to thwart the guards' attempts to cultivate despair. Mandela, along with his fellow inmates, hatched silent rebellions, using small acts of resistance to assert their humanity. From subtle gestures of solidarity, like sharing food or lending support during prayer, to resisting oppressive work schedules and demanding better treatment, these acts of defiance began to accumulate in significance.

The calls for justice and equality echoed louder than the clinking chains that bound their feet. Mandela's belief in non-violent resistance remained a cornerstone of his struggle, shaping how he and his comrades engaged with their oppressors. Instead of retaliating with violence, they sought to expose the brutality of the regime, turning the very acts meant to suppress them into a spotlight illuminating their plight. Mandela's steadfast refusal to bow to his captors resonated deeply throughout the prison walls, weaving a thread of resilience among them.

Critical to Mandela's survival was his connection to the outside world, even if through a series of limited interactions. Letters were the lifeline to his family and the outside political climate. Often, his wide-ranging correspondence acted not only as family updates but as vital conduits of hope that reminded him of the causes and people still fighting. He penned letters to his comrades outside prison, offering support and stipulating instructions for the liberation movement. Each letter served to fortify him, reaffirming his commitments to the ANC and the larger struggle for justice in South Africa.

The eventual recognition of his predicament brought international attention to the anti-apartheid struggle. Campaigns organized around the world began to draw attention to the plight of Mandela and his fellow prisoners, rallying support that transcended borders. His incarceration became a symbol of the oppression inherent in apartheid, amplifying calls for justice not only within South Africa but across the globe. Every solidarity rally, every call for his release, all ignited Mandela's conviction, instilling within him—and his fellow prisoners—a sense of purpose, shaping their collective identity as martyrs in the struggle for freedom.

In the labyrinth of Robben Island's oppressive walls, Mandela's spirit blossomed against the odds. He became not just a prisoner, but a man who fostered a resilient community grounded in friendship, activism, and collective vision. The fellowship forged between the men was as crucial to their survival as any physical sustenance, manifesting in moments of laughter, communal dreaming, and resistance. Through the bitterness of confinement, they managed to cultivate an oasis of hope, accentuated by their shared humanity and undying commitment to a future where freedom was not just a dream but an impending reality.

Life on Robben Island transformed Nelson Mandela from a fierce and able revolutionary into a symbol of resistance and resilience. The conditions may have sought to quench his spirit, but they instead fused it with an unbreakable resolve. Out of isolation and confinement arose a leader fortified by the bonds of fellowship, molded by adversity, and shaped by an unyielding pursuit of justice. With each dawn that broke over the rocky shores of Robben Island, Mandela's will and determination continued to burn bright, igniting the embers that would one day fuel the fires of change in South Africa.

Transformation through Adversity

The bleakness of Robben Island stood in stark contrast to the vibrant ideals Nelson Mandela had fought for throughout his youth. The prison, a mere seven kilometers from the Cape of Good Hope, was a complex of damp stone cells and harsh sunlight. Yet, within this purgatory, Mandela found the crucible necessary for his philosophical evolution. Imprisonment catalyzed a profound transformation, reshaping him from the vigorous young activist who once led a charge against apartheid into a contemplative leader capable of envisioning a new nation.

The first few years on Robben Island were characterized by a harsh routine, where the day-to-day existence was marked not only by physical confinement but by the psychological weight of hopelessness many prisoners succumbed to. For Mandela, however, this period became an opportunity for introspection. Removed from the tumultuous events of the outside world, he immersed himself in thoughts about justice, governance, and reconciliation. In the echoing silence of his cell, he wrestled with the weight of responsibility—a stark shift from his earlier years of passionate activism, where the urgency of undoing apartheid seemed far more straightforward.

It was here, in constant solitude, that Mandela began to dissect his beliefs and dissect the revolution he had embraced. His childhood had been steeped in ideals of African nationalism and liberation, yet confinement urged him to reconsider what true liberation meant. Mandela began reflecting not just on his own experiences and sufferings, but on the broader implications of his struggle for an entire nation.

Books became a lifeline during these years, providing him a window to the ideological world beyond the prison walls. Mandela's voracious reading could not simply be an escape; it became an instrument for transformation. He read everything from classic literature to political philosophies. In texts by Karl Marx, Friedrich Engels, and, notably, Mahatma Gandhi, he sought answers to questions that had lingered in his mind for years. The writings of these thinkers prompted Mandela to consider the nuances of struggles against oppression and how they played out in different socio-political contexts.

> "As I walked out the door toward my freedom, I knew if I didn't leave my bitterness and hatred behind, I'd still be in prison."
>
> — Nelson Mandela

Mandela's reflections led him down a more profound philosophical path, where his views on violence, justice, and the cost of revolution began to crystallize. This was not a retreat from his activism; rather, it was an expansion of it. He soon realized that the desire for immediate results could lead to cycles of violence that offered no sustainable solution.

As Mandela sat in his cell, he began to understand that every revolution—no matter how justified—had both costs and consequences. He began advocating more for negotiation and reconciliation over an unyielding quest for revenge, a strategy that alarmed some of his fellow inmates who continued to clamor for an armed struggle against the apartheid regime. This pivot marked a significant ideological shift in Mandela's outlook—a movement away from an absolute approach towards a more nuanced understanding of leadership and governance.

In conjunction with his readings, Mandela's discussions with fellow prisoners were invaluable in shaping his thoughts. Engaging in debates over the nature of freedom and justice, the importance of moral leadership soon surfaced as recurring themes. These conversations helped him appreciate the spectrum of human experiences and perspectives within the anti-apartheid movement, underscoring that liberation was not merely a political change but a moral and ethical quest.

As he contemplated the possibility of a post-apartheid South Africa, Mandela imagined a nation where justice meant everything—reconciliation and healing became pivotal parts of the narrative he would later propagate. He began to dream of a society not just free from oppression, but one defined by equality, dignity, and communal respect.

Through adversity, Mandela understood the transformative power of humility. Where once he might have viewed leadership as a position of dominance, he now saw it as service. True leaders, he concluded, were those who could inspire others through empathy and understanding. This expansive view began to take root during his long years of confinement.

The clarity reached during these years was not without its challenges. Embedded within Mandela's awakening was the realization that all revolutions demanded sacrifices. The message of forgiveness alongside the acknowledgment of past injustices began to resonate deeply with him. He drew increasingly from his Xhosa cultural roots, which emphasized collective identity and community healing, influencing his growing thoughts on how a new South Africa should emerge.

As Mandela continued to reflect on the costs of resistance and the complexities of leadership, he also pondered the personal sacrifices that had shaped his journey. He recognized the emotional toll of his imprisonment on his family and the communal anguish of countless South Africans. The unresolved pain of separation from his wife, Winnie, and the evolving nature of his relationship with his children weighed heavily upon him. He struck a delicate balance between personal sorrow and his ideological commitment, as he wrestled with the complicated legacy he would leave behind.

Despite the bleakness of Robben Island, Mandela's years there were imbued with purpose. The formidable challenges became a fertile ground for producing a more profound understanding of the human spirit. Through adversity, he unraveled his longing for liberation and transformed it into a pursuit for justice. His introspective journey eventually crystallized into a vision for a peaceful South Africa, a nation that could thrive through negotiation and consensus rather than further bloodshed.

Mandela's transformation was not merely a personal journey; it represented a larger shift in the ideology of leadership and revolution.

The ideas he cultivated within the prison walls began to cascade into the very fabric of the ANC's future endeavors. The framework for understanding conflict resolution, with an emphasis on reconciliation, encouraged others within the movement to reconsider their positions amidst the protracted struggle against apartheid.

Finally, the years spent on Robben Island molded Mandela into a formidable thinker. He emerged from that cell not just as a prisoner, but as a profound leader brimming with a philosophy of inclusivity and hope. The man who would one day lead a post-apartheid South Africa into an uncertain future was forged not in the fires of revolution but in the quiet contemplation of what it meant to be free. His reflections, born from shackles, would ultimately pave the way for a new nation eager to step onto the global stage with renewed purpose and spirit.

In conclusion, the story of Mandela's imprisonment is emblematic of the radical potential that lies within adversity. His years of introspection provided a roadmap not just for himself, but for an entire nation grappling with its identity and aspirations. The lessons of humility, the embrace of reconciliation, and the prioritization of moral leadership transformed a mere revolutionary into a sage— capable of guiding South Africa towards a vision not only steeped in freedom but nurturing a collective memory of courage and hope.

The Voice of Resistance

In the dim, inhospitable surroundings of Robben Island, Nelson Mandela emerged not merely as an inmate but as a beacon of hope—a living symbol of resistance against the horrendous injustices of apartheid. While the prison's walls were designed to silence, they inadvertently amplified his voice, allowing it to resonate beyond the island and into the hearts of millions. His ability to inspire the downtrodden within the prison and rally international support exemplified the dual role he played as both a political prisoner and an emblematic leader of the anti-apartheid movement.

Mandela's resilience in captivity was remarkable. He was imprisoned for 27 years, forced to endure severe hardships, forced labor, and dehumanization. Yet, even in these dark tunnels of despair, his spirit remained unbroken. His letters became the lifeline to the outside world, a conduit through which he shared not only his personal experiences but also the broader struggle of his people. By penning his thoughts, reflections, and unwavering convictions to his comrades, he managed to keep the flame of resistance alive.

The correspondence that Mandela engaged in was not merely an exercise in self-expression; it was an act of defiance. Each letter he wrote was imbued with powerful messages. He crafted words that motivated his peers and galvanized support, reminding them that the struggle for liberation was not isolated to the confines of Robben Island. His letters would go on to become intrinsic to the narrative of resistance, inspiring demonstrations and protests that echoed far beyond South Africa's borders.

One of the most powerful examples of his correspondence revolved around the latter part of the 1960s. During this period, Mandela's insights into the situation in South Africa grew more sophisticated. He focused on articulating the plight of black South Africans and outlined strategies to bolster support for their liberation. His letters were resonating within the ANC, as the leadership sought to galvanize their ranks and rally support against the apartheid government.

Mandela's words served as both a reflection of the mounting anger against the regime and a call to arms for those still fighting on the outside. He made it clear—his imprisonment was not a mark of defeat but rather a symbol of struggle. In one poignant letter to the ANC leadership, he articulated, "The struggle is not yet over. We must remain resolute, united, and unwavering in our quest for a just society. The world is watching, and we must not fail them." Words like these forged a common purpose among scattered activists, reaffirming their resolve amid desperate times.

As Mandela's influence burgeoned, so too did the international anti-apartheid movement. The realization that Mandela was a key figure in this struggle catalyzed international campaigns aimed at securing his release. Outside of South Africa, countless people were drawn into the fight for freedom, ignited by stories of Mandela's spirit and determination. Public protests across the globe were organized— rallies became vibrant spectacles where thousands of voices chanted for his release and justice for the oppressed.

A notable campaign emerged in the early 1980s, the "Free Nelson Mandela" movement, which served as a focal point for global protest against apartheid. It united disparate groups—from student organizations to trade unions—creating a choir of voices that reverberated worldwide. Here, Mandela's mere name became synonymous with liberation, galvanizing public sentiment as citizens joined hands in solidarity against the apartheid regime. The banner of resistance, emblazoned with his name, became a common sight on placards spanning city squares in London, Paris, and New York.

Among countless protestors, the resolve was palpable. The heartfelt chants of "Free Nelson Mandela!" ignited a fervor that resonated with those who felt an intrinsic connection to his struggle, directly or indirectly affected by oppression. In music, art, and poetry, Mandela's name manifested as a powerful silence-breaker, amplifying the struggles of the marginalized and showcasing the shared humanity that underpinned the struggle for justice.

Globally recognized artists rallied to the issue. Music became a significant vehicle, with acts like U2, Joan Baez, and many others creating songs that paid homage to Mandela while igniting awareness around the injustices plaguing South Africa. The song "Free Nelson Mandela" by The Specials caught fire in the public domain, transforming his name into an anthem of hope. This widespread artistic expression brought a new layer of awareness to the anti-apartheid struggle and turned Mandela into a figure that transcended the boundaries of nationalism—an embodiment of universal ideals of freedom and justice.

Simultaneously, the call for Mandela's release carried implications on political landscapes worldwide. With every protest, every letter published, and every artist who infused his legacy into their artistry, the international community's pressure on the South African government intensified. Countries began to adopt sanctions, and divestment campaigns gained momentum, leading multinational corporations to reconsider their relationships with the apartheid regime.

The impact of these campaigns extended well beyond mere slogans. They catalyzed action, and over time, grassroot movements emerged. Activists across continents sent messages to their governments demanding the end of apartheid, driving a wedge between the administration of South Africa and the will of its people—both at home and abroad. The unyielding determination of these campaigners was driven in part by the powerful image of Mandela, a man enduring unimaginable hardships yet rising as a symbol of hope.

Yet, Mandela was not merely a passive image; he was instrumental in guiding the movement from within the prison walls. His letters frequently emphasized the ideals of unity and reconciliation in a fractured society. Even while imprisoned, he continually urged his comrades against violent retaliations that could deepen racial divisions. In one letter, he wrote, "We must remember that our struggle is not purely about our freedom. It is also about creating a just society, a society where all can coexist and thrive, regardless of race." Such wisdom accentuated his role as a thoughtful leader, reinforcing his ability to inspire hope while urging prudence.

> **"There is no passion to be found playing small — in settling for a life that is less than the one you are capable of living."**
>
> — Nelson Mandela

Perhaps one of the most significant letters written during this period was addressed to President P.W. Botha in 1989, in which he made an impassioned appeal for moderation and a peaceful transition. While many anticipated attempts for violence from within the ANC, Mandela sought a path defined by dialogue and mutual understanding. His commitment to peace was emblematic of the stance he sought to embody as a leader, ensuring that the world knew his imprisonment would not wear down nor harden his heart against potential reconciliation.

Amidst the rise of activism, the role of the media played a pivotal role in amplifying Mandela's messages. International news outlets covered protests, global campaigns, and the harrowing tales surrounding Robben Island. As the public became increasingly aware of the gulf between apartheid's ideals and the lived experiences of South Africans, Mandela's story unlocked empathy in ways that transformed indifference into a chorus of commitment against racial tyranny. Newspaper articles chronicled the legends surrounding Mandela's resolve, reinforcing that while he was unjustly imprisoned, he was anything but silenced.

The stories of unity sparked by the "Free Nelson Mandela" campaigns helped to build momentum for protests, rallies, and solidarity events. As citizens in countries like the United States, Britain, and various nations across Europe joined forces, they sent a clear message that they could not turn a blind eye to injustice. People rallied with fervor, transcending borders—a diverse collective continuously reflecting the spirit of humanity embodied in Mandela's continued strength.

In the final years of Mandela's imprisonment, as tensions climbed not only in South Africa but globally, how Mandela's name was invoked evolved from an emblem of resistance to one of reconciliation. This transition echoed through protests around the world, as people no longer shouted solely for his freedom, but began to envision the future of South Africa—a post-apartheid narrative that sought to bridge divides and foster healing.

As anticipation of Mandela's release built, so too did the momentum surrounding global campaigns. His eventual release on February 11, 1990, marked a seismic shift—not just for South Africa but for the world. The protests that had surged forth around his imprisonment transitioned into celebrations—a testament to the strength and unity of those who had rallied behind his cause. It was a confirmation that even in an oppressive society, hope could endure, and resistance could triumph.

After his release, Mandela continued to be a symbol of unity, carrying the legacy of resilience etched into his voice throughout his incarceration. His newfound position allowed him to directly advocate for peace and reconciliation, continuing to inspire others and cementing his role as a figure of resistance while laying the groundwork for a new South Africa. Addressing a crowd of jubilant supporters, he proclaimed, "I stand here before you not as a prophet but as a humble servant of you, the people. Your struggles have brought me here today, and our collective journey is just beginning."

Mandela's trajectory from an imprisoned revolutionary to a statesman revealed the profound teaching moments of his life. Those years spent behind bars not only encapsulated his resistance against oppression but also his commitment to shaping a future built on compassion and understanding. Through his letters and his eventual reunification with the movement, Mandela embodied a duality rarely achieved: he evolved from symbol to leader, championing the voices of those who fought alongside him, who endured the suffering of apartheid, and who dreamed of liberation.

His legacy, fortified through the echoes of resistance that resonated long after his release, endures—a reminder of how one voice, rising in the face of oppression, can inspire change across borders, languages, and ideologies. As such, Mandela remains a profound reminder that within the chains of oppression lies the strength to rise, resist, and ultimately transform the world.

The Symphony of Negotiation

*"Courageous people do not fear
forgiving, for the sake of peace."*

— Nelson Mandela

The Tipping Point

In the late 1980s, South Africa stood on the precipice of monumental change. The apartheid regime, a system rooted in racial segregation and oppression, faced increasing scrutiny both from within its borders and on the international stage. For decades, the policies of the National Party had enforced strict racial classifications, resulting in disenfranchisement, economic disparity, and social strife that tore the country apart. However, as the winds of change began to blow across the nation, a collective spirit of resistance sparked by years of struggle and sacrifice initiated a powerful movement toward liberation.

As civil unrest erupted, protests became a frequent occurrence. Townships were engulfed in violence, as activists and ordinary citizens alike defied the oppressive regime that had classified them as second-class citizens. Institutionalized racism incited outrage, leading to a series of strikes, protests, and unprecedented riots. The South African landscape was marked by turmoil, but beneath the surface lay an undeniable current of hope; a hope that was becoming increasingly infectious across the nation.

Internationally, economic sanctions and disinvestment campaigns were gaining momentum. Countries around the globe were applying pressure on the South African government, demanding an end to apartheid. The tide was shifting, forcing the National Party to reckon with the cracks that were beginning to form within their all-powerful facade. The world watched closely as it became evident that apartheid was no longer tenable; its internal tensions were bubbling over, threatening the very existence of the regime.

> **"For to be free is not merely to cast off one's chains, but to live in a way that respects and enhances the freedom of others."**
>
> — Nelson Mandela

Amidst this political maelstrom, one individual remained an unwavering symbol of resistance: Nelson Mandela. Having spent over twenty-seven years incarcerated, Mandela emerged from prison on February 11, 1990, as a figure that transcended the struggles he had endured. His release from the bleak confines of Robben Island injected a new vitality into the liberation movement and solidified his position as the face of hope for millions of South Africans longing for liberation.

Mandela's release was not just a personal triumph; it constituted a seismic shift in the political landscape of South Africa. The anticipation surrounding this event was palpable, reverberating through communities that had long awaited this moment of reckoning. Crowds gathered in the streets, their cheers echoing with fervor as they awaited the return of their leader. His first public address as a free man demanded the dismantling of apartheid and the commencement of negotiations for a peaceful resolution. "I stand before you, not as a prophet, but as a humble servant of you, the people. Your tireless and heroic struggle has brought us to this moment," Mandela proclaimed, forging an unbreakable bond with the masses who had stood steadfast in their fight against oppression.

In the years leading to his release, Mandela had transformed from a fiery revolutionary into a calculated strategist, fully cognizant of the pivotal role negotiation would play in the transition toward a post-apartheid South Africa. The external and internal pressures on the apartheid government had created a fertile ground for dialogue, and Mandela seized this moment with intention. No longer merely an activist, he became a key player in the game of politics, realizing that to ensure a peaceful future, he must engage with both allies and adversaries alike.

The ensuing negotiations with the apartheid government were fraught with general uncertainty and tension. For the National Party, the crumbling structures of apartheid also presented an existential threat; they were aware that their grip on power was loosening, and the possibility of civil war loomed ominously if a peaceful transition was not achieved. Concessions would need to be made, and the architects of the apartheid regime were forced to rethink their legitimacy in the face of increasingly organized resistance and mounting international pressure.

As Mandela engaged with adversaries at the negotiating table, an intricate dance unfolded. On one hand, there existed a shared understanding that a solution was essential to avoid further bloodshed; on the other hand, stark ideological differences revealed sharp divisions. The ANC sought not only political power but also structural transformations that would address the deep-seated inequalities established by apartheid. Simultaneously, the National Party was reluctant to relinquish the stranglehold it had maintained on governance for decades.

A recognition emerged within the ranks of both parties, grounded in the painful lessons history had taught: any agreement reached would have to provide a framework that went beyond mere political transition. Trust would be paramount, and tensions would rise and fall as both sides navigated the common ground that needed to be established.

Each meeting bore the weight of the nation's hopes and fears. As key actors across the political spectrum began to congregate, the conversation shifted from one of animosity to one of tentative cooperation. The dynamics of power evolved as Mandela often transformed adversarial exchanges into opportunities for mutual understanding. He recognized that meaningful dialogue required both a willingness to listen and an openness to engage constructively.

The role of international actors proved pivotal during this time. Nations around the globe observed with rapt attention, not merely as spectators but as participants in the building of a new South Africa. A chorus of support emerged, sent through various means—economic aid, moral support, and diplomatic engagements. The world was inextricably linked to the outcome of the negotiations as a new era seemed inevitable.

Participants found themselves beset by the enormity of their responsibility to their respective constituencies. Mandela understood that it was not simply about arriving at an agreement; it was about crafting a legacy that would endure. Simultaneously, his opponents in negotiations began to understand that embracing change was essential for their own survival, lest they be trampled under the weight of history. The intricacies of this new political landscape were becoming clearer, with Mandela positioned at the helm as a mediator who could transcend the ruptured divides of the past.

As negotiations progressed, the symbolism of Mandela's persona continued to reinforce the hope for reconciliation. His unwavering moral compass became both a guiding principle for the ANC's actions and a fundamental element in the negotiation process itself. By cultivating relationships across party lines and emphasizing the importance of inclusivity, Mandela sought to build an atmosphere wherein fear could give way to trust. Recognizing that leaders in opposing camps were subject to their own pressures and fears, he endeavored to create an environment conducive to genuine dialogue.

The shifting sands of South African politics informed the trajectory of the negotiations. People on both sides of the political spectrum expressed anxieties regarding potential outcomes—but as the months passed, it was clear that compromise was no longer an abstract concept. It was a necessity. Guided by Mandela's vision and leadership, the ANC began to articulate the foundation of policies that would undergird a new South Africa, reflecting the aspirations of all its people.

As 1991 came and went, the negotiations were punctuated by milestones that fueled the urgency for progress. Key events such as the formation of the Convention for a Democratic South Africa

(CODESA) represented a groundbreaking platform for reaching consensus among diverse factions. The political atmosphere remained charged, yet elusive; negotiations were often stalled by mistrust, yet spurred by a collective desire for meaningful change.

In the end, the tipping point lay not merely in Mandela's release from prison but in the courage displayed by individuals on both sides to engage in honest conversations about the future of their nation. It was a willingness to confront past injustices and envision a shared future that ultimately created the framework for negotiation. The sacrifices made across generations for the dream of freedom ultimately coalesced in a powerful narrative that transcended the divide of race, ideology, and class.

As discussions progressed, the global community remained vigilant, cautiously optimistic yet anxious about what the future held. Mandela's release had been the catalyst; now, the world watched as the journey of negotiation unfolded, propelled by hope but mired in the complexities of human history. Despite the uncertainties that lay ahead, a drumbeat of conviction rang clear across the land: the desire for a united South Africa was resonating louder than ever before, and the negotiations epitomized not just a political endeavor, but a collective moral imperative.

As negotiators sought to reconcile opposing interests, the realities of life in South Africa served as a constant testament to the need for reconciliation. Townships filled with voices of the marginalized, urging their leaders to remember those who had sacrificed everything in the years of struggle. In the hearts of many, there existed an unyielding determination that apartheid's legacy must be transformed into an abiding promise of justice. Mandela's ability to channel this collective sentiment into a transformative vision became a hallmark of his leadership.

As we delve deeper into the complexities surrounding the negotiations that defined this pivotal moment in South African history, it becomes clear that the journey toward a new reality was paved with profound challenges, remarkable courage, and the unwavering human spirit. Each exchange at the negotiating table propelled the country closer to a watershed moment: a majestic opportunity for reconciliation, forged through dialogue and mutual respect—a possibility that Mandela structured with strategic grace.

In walking through this labyrinthine process of negotiation, the dynamics of power shifted; a new recognition emerged of the interconnectedness of all people in shaping the nation's future. With it came the realization that the only sustainable victory would be one that embraced the legitimate aspirations of all South Africans.

Thus, as the negotiations unfolded in that turbulent landscape, a dual realization emerged: freedom and justice would only manifest through collaboration. In this symphony of negotiation, every note, every word, and every concession played a role in composing the harmonies of a future grounded in the principles of equality, unity, and hope. And at the center of this evolving narrative stood Nelson Mandela, embodying a vision that would ultimately help to redefine not only South Africa but the essence of leadership itself.

Negotiating the Future

The negotiations leading to the end of apartheid in South Africa marked a transformative chapter not only for the country but also for the global narrative around the struggle for freedom and justice. As Nelson Mandela emerged from twenty-seven years of imprisonment, the landscape was precarious. The apartheid government was crumbling under pressure from both internal resistance and international sanctions. Mandela's release in February 1990 was not just a victory for him personally but also a symbol of hope for millions of South Africans yearning for equality. This moment set the stage for a series of negotiations that would determine the future of South Africa.

Upon his release, Mandela embraced a dual role: he was not only the figurehead of the ANC but also a strategist who had to navigate the treacherous waters of South African politics. The interim years leading up to the 1994 elections were fraught with tension, violence, and uncertainty. For Mandela, the task at hand involved ushering in a new era of democratic governance while simultaneously ensuring the safety and security of all South Africans—black and white.

The negotiations officially began with the start of formal talks in mid-1990, shortly after Mandela's release. Initially, the process was complicated by deeply entrenched mistrust between the ANC and the National Party (NP) government, led by then-President F.W. de Klerk. The NP had been the architect of apartheid and was not perceived to be genuinely committed to change. As political discussions commenced, countless hurdles emerged, presenting a complex challenge for Mandela and his negotiators.

One major hurdle in these negotiations was the deep-seated belief among many members of the ANC that they had the moral high ground. The ANC was seen as the legitimate voice of the oppressed, while the apartheid government was viewed as an oppressive regime with no credibility. Yet, Mandela understood the necessity of engaging in dialogue with those who had long been seen as adversaries. He recognized that without engaging the NP, the prospect of a peaceful transition was slim.

In one of their early meetings, Mandela faced a pivotal moment. During a negotiation session at the World Trade Centre in Kempton

Park, tensions flared as both sides grappled with their narratives. De Klerk was aware that the NP needed to maintain some level of power to protect the interest of the white minority, while ANC leaders were adamantly pushing for a complete dismantling of apartheid structures. Mandela intervened, reminding both parties of the overarching goal: a peaceful, democratic South Africa. "We are not here to negotiate power for ourselves, but freedom for our people," he stated, setting a tone of reconciliation rather than revenge.

> **"Do not judge me by my successes, judge me by how many times I fell and got back up again."**
>
> — Nelson Mandela

Despite Mandela's diplomatic approach, the negotiations were met with fierce opposition from various factions. While the ANC sought unity and peace, splinter groups within the organization held differing views. The ANC was not a monolith; it encompassed a spectrum of ideologies, from moderates who favored negotiation to hardliners who believed that armed struggle should not cease until apartheid had been completely dismantled. Leaders such as Chris Hani, the head of the South African Communist Party, openly challenged Mandela's conciliatory strategies, arguing that the ANC was conceding too much in the name of peace. These internal pressures weighed heavily on Mandela, complicating his efforts to maintain a unified front.

On the other side, the NP was contending with its own factions. As Mandela and De Klerk engaged in negotiations, the Afrikaner nationalist sentiment surged within segments of the white community. Many whites saw the negotiations as a sellout, fearing for their safety and future in a democratic South Africa. The violent attacks by the right-wing groups, particularly the AWB (Afrikaner Resistance Movement), underscored the palpable tensions. The assassination of ANC leader Chris Hani in April 1993 brought South Africa to the brink of civil war, amplifying fears and anxieties on both sides.

Amid these pressures, Mandela maintained a steadfast commitment to peaceful resolution. He understood that the power to overcome the past lay in empathy and understanding, not vengeance. In addressing a gathering of the ANC in May 1993, Mandela proclaimed, "To be free is not merely to cast off one's chains, but to live in a way that respects and enhances the freedom of others." His words were not just philosophical; they were a strategic call to action aimed at preserving peace during a turbulent period.

The formal negotiations encountered many technical challenges as well. Issues such as land restitution, property rights, and the establishment of a new constitution required thorough examination. The negotiations revolved around a constitutional framework, raising the question of how to enshrine equality and justice for all South Africans, while also reflecting the diversity of the nation. In 1992 the Convention for a Democratic South Africa (CODESA) was created to facilitate these discussions, bringing together various political organizations to forge a consensus.

Amid these complexities, Mandela sought to forge alliances. He reached out to moderate, influential figures within the NP who were also keen to end apartheid. These connections were crucial in facilitating honest dialogue, enabling trust-building across party lines. Mandela's ability to engage in negotiations while cultivating relationships with key figures like de Klerk exemplified his diplomatic prowess. He sought to humanize his adversaries, seeing beyond their political positions to their vulnerabilities and fears.

Throughout these negotiations, international support played a significant role. The worldwide anti-apartheid movement galvanized public opinion in favor of the ANC and placed pressure on the NP to negotiate in good faith. Foreign governments, international organizations, and civil society groups offered their support for a peaceful transition, providing funding and resources to strengthen the ANC's negotiating position. The global stage was abuzz with anticipation as South Africa became synonymous with hope for freedom and democracy.

In the face of increasing tension and violence, both parties understood the urgency of reaching an agreement. Mandela's leadership shone as he demonstrated his capacity to make difficult decisions. He knew that appeasing internal dissenters without compromising the negotiations was a delicate balancing act, but one that he had to maneuver with skill.

The negotiations culminated in 1994 when the first democratic elections took place, culminating a long struggle for freedom. Mandela's ascension to the presidency signified the triumph of the ideals of justice and equality. Yet, the journey leading to the elections was mired in complexity, as Mandela had to manage various expectations.

Despite this monumental achievement, the negotiations had left many in the ANC—especially the hardliners—feeling that compromises had been made at too high a cost. The decision to not pursue retribution against apartheid officials was particularly contentious. Mandela sought to ensure stability and peace, advocating for the establishment of the Truth and Reconciliation Commission (TRC), aimed at addressing past human rights violations and promoting healing. This move, while strategically important for societal stability, stood as a testament to the conflicted views within the ANC regarding justice and accountability.

The aftermath of the negotiations revealed that while the transition to democracy was celebrated, the fallout included an ongoing struggle to address socioeconomic disparities. Mandela's commitment to reconciliation was admirable, but simultaneously, the long-term structural inequalities persisted, leading to ongoing discontent among communities that had been part of the liberation struggle.

In reflection, the negotiations that unfolded from 1990 to 1994 were marked by challenges, triumphs, and sacrifices. The balancing act that Mandela performed was nothing short of extraordinary—in navigating internal dissent, external pressures, and deeply polarizing issues. While Mandela's role as a negotiator is often celebrated, it's essential to critique the resultant framework and acknowledge the lingering complexity of South Africa's democratic project.

The Agreement

On a cool autumn day in 1993, a defining moment unfolded in the dark history of South Africa. The air was thick with anticipation as Nelson Mandela and F.W. de Klerk stepped into a negotiating room, their pasts heavy with the weight of decades of struggle and conflict. After years of brutal apartheid, marked by violence and segregation, the stakes had never been higher. The world watched as these two unlikely leaders, representing the oppressed and the oppressors, prepared to chart a new course for their nation—one that could ultimately bring an end to centuries of racial injustice.

The negotiations leading to this agreement were not merely the result of strategic diplomacy; they emerged from a deep-rooted sense of urgency. For decades, the African National Congress (ANC) had fought tirelessly for liberation, while the apartheid regime clung to its power through violent repression. The landscape of South Africa had begun to tremble under the force of growing discontent. Protests erupted, townships were ablaze, and a groundswell of activism filled the streets, echoing the cries for justice.

Mandela's release from prison in February 1990 ignited a flicker of hope in the hearts of millions. However, it quickly became apparent that the road to reconciliation would be fraught with difficulties. Each side entered the discussions with their own perceptions of justice, power, and the future of South Africa. While the ANC envisioned a democratic society where all voices would be heard, the National Party sought to safeguard their interests amid a rapidly changing political landscape. This stark contrast shaped every interaction.

As the dates approached for the agreement to be finalized, tension permeated the atmosphere. Supporters of both sides were anxious and uncertain, fearing that the process could unravel or, conversely, emerge with a solution too paltry to satisfy the aspirations of the populace. Around the country, communities held their breath, waiting for a glimpse of hope amidst their despair.

On the morning of April 17, 1993, the atmosphere was electric as Mandela, with his iconic smile, and De Klerk, composed yet visibly tense, stood before a congregation of eager journalists and international representatives. The two leaders were set to announce the framework for a new South Africa, a liberated nation that would no longer be shackled by the oppressive laws of apartheid. The anticipation was palpable as they presented their proposal: a gradual transition towards democracy.

The agreement called for the establishment of a new constitution that would ensure equal rights for every South African, irrespective of race. It aimed to lay the groundwork for a multi-party system in which the ANC and other parties could freely participate in a democratic process. The emotions in the room swept across ecstatic pride and sobering disbelief, revealing the complexities of human emotion in this pivotal moment. Members of the ANC jubilantly embraced, while others, skeptics of the process, held their breath in worry, uncertain of the true intentions behind the smiles of their erstwhile oppressors.

On the ground level, the news was met with mixed reactions. In townships, drumbeats filled the air as vendors sold celebratory paraphernalia. Jubilations erupted in the streets as children danced, embodying the hope of a brighter future. Yet, within the same communities, groups of disillusioned activists voiced skepticism, fearing that Mandela's negotiations signaled a betrayal of the revolutionary principles that had fueled their movement.

Public perception during this period was a tapestry of excitement, hope, and skepticism. For many, Mandela had become synonymous with justice and reconciliation. Others questioned whether the compromises made would indeed lead to a meaningful transformation or merely substitute one form of oppression for another. The ANC was thrust into a challenging position—fielding expectations that their leader had promised liberation while also navigating a tide of voices claiming betrayal. The balance of emotions was fragile, and the agreement's implications began to unfold beyond the borders of South Africa.

On a global scale, South Africans were no longer the only ones watching this transition. The world held its breath, observing both the risks and the potential triumphs of negotiations. The end of apartheid reverberated through the telecommunication lines to nations steeped in their struggles for freedom. For many activists around the globe, the peaceful negotiations in South Africa became a beacon of hope. The agreement symbolized a landmark shift in paradigms, affirming the possibility of resolving conflicts through dialogue rather than violence.

Yet, critiques began to emerge almost immediately. Some analysts dissected the agreement, arguing that it was a product of appeasement rather than true transformation. Detractors posited that the deal made too many concessions to the former ruling party, leaving intact vestiges of apartheid power structures. Key questions arose about land reform, economic redistributions, and the genuine capacity of the new government to address the chasms of inequality that had been a product of decades of oppression.

The grim realities of lingering poverty, systemic racism, and economic disparity reminded the nation that the struggle was far from over. For many, the optimism of the agreement was overshadowed by fears of "business as usual" for the elite while the marginalized continued to bear the brunt of societal injustices. Voices of discontent echoed within ANC ranks and among civil society members, as slogans that once rallied individuals towards revolution morphed into expressions depicting betrayal.

In the weeks following the agreement's announcement, public opinion continued to fluctuate. The initial exhilaration was met by waves of anxiety as the populace began to grapple with the practical implications of the agreement. Following a notorious spate of violence against communities perceived as supportive of apartheid, the atmosphere oscillated between jubilation and panic. How would the new leadership navigate these treacherous waters?

As Mandela and the ANC readied for elections in 1994, they faced accusations of having sold out. This sentiment found voice through protests in various enclaves of South African society. Some of the very individuals who had borne the brunt of apartheid's brutality now feared being cast aside while their leaders climbed into government. The betrayal narrative gained momentum and space in both critical and mainstream circles, further complicating the beautiful tapestry that the agreement aimed to stitch together.

"It always seems impossible until it's done."

— Nelson Mandela

The implications of the agreement extended far beyond South Africa's borders. The international community recognized the possibility of political transformation through negotiation, challenging long-held paradigms about power dynamics and conflicts. Countries grappling with their forms of oppression began to look towards South Africa as a case study. Would the lessons learned here apply to their struggles? The negotiations proved that, where invested actors engaged in dialogue, viable solutions could emerge.

What began to unfurl on a global scale was a newfound discourse that re-evaluated long-standing assumptions about power and resistance. Emerging economies, liberation movements, and various human rights organizations reflected on the lessons learned from South Africa's engagement—highlighting the importance of patience, strategy, and compromise through a collective vision.

However, as time unfolded, so too did critiques questioning the efficacy of the agreement. The expectation that a new political architecture could effectively address the grave inequities left in apartheid's wake soon collided with the harsh reality of governance. As the ANC transitioned from liberation movement to party in power, the challenges of transforming a divided society became strikingly apparent. The anticipated utopia became a battleground where promises clashed with realities, forcing reflection on the efficacy of leadership in navigating complex social change.

In the years following the negotiated agreement, the fluctuating public perceptions served as a reminder of the dualities inherent in the political landscape. Mandela and the ANC, once venerated as champions of liberation, faced a sobering reality as disillusionment began surfacing among their early supporters. Conflicts emerged between progress and expectations, as the social fabric struggled to reconcile promises of freedom with on-the-ground realities of life in a new democracy.

Mandela's legacy was further muddied by public debates that flared around issues such as land redistribution and economic inequity. The negotiations that paved the way for a democratic South Africa were admirable, yet how they translated into practice became the subject of intense scrutiny. Once venerated, he now often stood accused of failing to address the very concerns that drove the struggle for liberation.

In reflecting on the impact of the agreement, it is essential to recognize that compromises often come at a cost. The historical moment was not only a victory for freedom but also a testament to the messy realities of leadership amid transition. Mandela's journey through reconciliation revealed the complexities of balancing idealism with pragmatism, and the weight of accountability that has followed him remains part of the South African narrative.

As discussions continue around Mandela's legacy, centered within the framework of the agreement, it emerges that the path he carved was not a linear one. It contested the ideals of revolution while exploring the weighty realities of governance. The trajectory from battle to negotiation turned South Africa into a remarkable story of resilience, fraught with tension between aspirations for equality and confronting harsh socioeconomic truths.

The agreement signed in 1993 stands as a profound moment in history—one where an ancient cycle of oppression met the prospect of hope. Yet, as history would continue to reveal, the unraveling of that narrative would not adhere strictly to the ideals penned in the agreement. Beyond the applause and celebrations, the chronic dilemmas of a divided society invited ongoing reflections on what true liberation means in the face of reality.

The dual nature of hope and discontent continues to shape the South African narrative, underscoring the complex legacies that emerged from this historic agreement. As the nation moves forward, it carries with it the collective memory of a people who refused to surrender their dreams, deftly weaving the challenges of the past into the aspirations of the present.

Betrayal or Balance?

*"Reconciliation does not mean forgetting
or trying to bury the pain of conflict, but
that reconciliation means working together
to correct the legacy of past injustice."*

— Nelson Mandela

The Compromise

The journey toward democracy in South Africa was riddled with difficult choices and painful compromises, particularly in the waning days of apartheid. Nelson Mandela, revered as a symbol of hope and freedom, faced monumental decisions during this critical time. The compromises he made reverberated through the political landscape, sparking debates about loyalty, idealism, and the very essence of leadership. As the first black president of the nation,

Mandela's choices not only shaped his legacy but also altered the course of the African National Congress (ANC) and the collective hopes and dreams of millions of South Africans.

In the late 1980s, apartheid had begun showing signs of fracture. Internally, the movement for freedom surged, featuring a rising tide of strikes, protests, and acts of defiance against an oppressive regime. Externally, mounting international pressure and sanctions from the global community made the continuance of apartheid untenable. Yet, amid this turmoil, negotiations were poised to commence, and Mandela's role as both a leader and negotiator put him at a crossroads, where each decision carried immense weight.

> **"Without education, your children can never really meet the challenges they will face."**
>
> — Nelson Mandela

Mandela has often stated that the time spent in prison was not merely a period of confinement but a school of life that offered invaluable lessons on patience, resilience, and the complexities of leadership. Once released in 1990, he found himself in a position that demanded more than just tenacity; he had to navigate a political minefield full of hopes, fears, and expectations not only from the black populace but also from the white minority, the apartheid government, and international actors.

The very foundation of the negotiations would rest on a multitude of compromises, transforming fierce revolutionary rhetoric into the language of diplomacy. The ANC leadership, guided by Mandela's vision, embarked on discussions that would eventually yield a new constitution and the promise of multiracial democracy. However, these discussions came with substantial sacrifices. The idea of a total break with the apartheid regime transformed into a palette of negotiations laced with concessions that some perceived as betrayal.

Skepticism within the ANC ranks centered around what some termed a surrender to the oppressor. For many hardened activists who had fought against the injustices of apartheid, the compromises felt like a betrayal of the blood spilled during the long fight for freedom. The notion that the ANC would engage in dialogue rather than fight until the bitter end incited passionate debates. The harsh realities of negotiating with a government that had oppressed the masses for decades demanded not only compromises but also an acknowledgment of the necessity for pragmatism in the face of overwhelming challenges.

In this context, the voices of discontent within activist circles spoke to a profound sense of betrayal. Some leaders echoed the sentiment that the revolutionary ideals upheld by the ANC were diluted in the name of political expediency. The prospect of peace was weighted heavily against the backdrop of sacrifices made. Promises to dismantle apartheid had been met with concessions on issues such as land redistribution and economic reform—a duality that left many cornered in their faith in Mandela.

The ANC's policies around compromise also reflected broader ideological divides within the organization. Younger leaders sought aggressive measures and radical reforms, while older stalwarts, many of whom had seen the bleakest times of apartheid, recognized the critical importance of gradual change to maintain stability. The dialogue between these factions was fraught with tension, but ultimately it was Mandela who skillfully mediated, crafting a narrative of unity from discord.

Public sentiment around these compromises was decidedly mixed. For many, Mandela's capacity to broker peace was commendable—a collective sigh of relief swept across the nation as negotiations progressed towards ended violence and societal ruptures. People celebrated the prospect of a democratic South Africa. Yet within this joy, skepticism persisted. The general populace grappled with the fear that the compromises negotiated might lead to a continuation of economic inequality and a failure to address the systematic injustices entrenched in the nation's fabric. Activists demanded immediate action; relief and justice needed to replace waiting and negotiations.

Mandela's approach to these compromises extended beyond mere political strategy; it was born of a deep-seated belief in reconciliation. His philosophy of forgiveness imparted to many South Africans an understanding that enduring peace required more than just punitive measures against former oppressors. However, the potential zenith of his leadership was not without its costs.

The socio-political environment was charged with uncertainty. Although negotiations were hailed as the pathway to liberation, they also ignited fears of betrayal among those who felt that not enough was done to address the socio-economic disparities wrought by apartheid. The compromise became synonymous with perceptions of weakness—of conceding too much to a regime that had unjustly ruled for decades. As frustrations grew, Mandela remained resolute, reiterating that negotiation was essential for long-term stability and that lifetimes of conflict had not yielded resolutions akin to those predicted through dialogue.

The compromises made during this transition had immediate effects. The ANC emerged from the negotiations with a fragile peace in a tumultuous landscape. The multiracial elections of 1994, where Mandela was voted in as president, symbolized hope, yet the divisions persisted. The expectations surrounding the ANC's governance were astronomical; a vast electorate sought transformation overnight. However, the realities of economic management and reconciliation posed formidable challenges that could not be resolved through political will alone.

Mandela's strategy entailed prioritizing nation-building over widespread vengeance. This approach included the establishment of the Truth and Reconciliation Commission, a body designed to address the atrocities committed during the apartheid years. While intended to foster healing, it also led to harsh criticism. Detractors viewed the Commission as a platform that allowed perpetrators of violence to evade justice, obscuring the realities faced by countless victims of apartheid.

Long-term effects of the compromises made during these negotiations manifested in various ways. Economically, while apartheid laws dismantled, the legacy of unequal socio-economic structures endured, constraining the government's capacity to deliver radical reforms. Mandela's leadership, steeped in ideals of reconciliation, had to grapple with a reality where economic stability clashed with aspirations for equality. The compromises struck a delicate balance that preserved peace but limited revolutionary change, underscoring politics' uncompromising nature where idealism often falters.

The discourse around betrayal in this context became embedded in the national identity. For many South Africans, Mandela's legacy evolved from a singular narrative into a more nuanced tapestry, interwoven with stories of hope, courage, and discontent. The very compromises that brought about democracy redefined perceptions of leadership. An emerging consensus recognized leadership's complexities; it was not solely rooted in actions on public stages but rather in the wrestle between ideologies, the passion for change, and the painful recognition that true transformation often requires sacrifices.

Mandela's willingness to embrace negotiation over violent confrontation marked a broader evolution of political leadership in Africa and beyond. His choices illustrated that sometimes, surrendering a piece of one's vision can lead to greater accomplishments than endless circulation of violence and unrest. His legacy became one where compromise is both a means and an end, a powerful tool in the hands of those willing to engage in the arduous journey toward collective healing.

However, as the years rolled on, critiques of Mandela's decisions increasingly spotlighted perceptions of failure to deliver on promises. The Mahatma Gandhi-inspired concept of non-violent resistance that characterized his early years morphed into a more pragmatic approach underscored by the pragmatic realities of governance. Such shifts were met with disappointment by the very electorate that had placed their hopes in him. The dreams of a radical reconstruction of society collided with the complex socio-economic realities that constantly shadowed his fledgling government.

In analyzing Mandela's compromises, it becomes clear that the essence of his leadership resides less in decisions devoid of conflict and more in those decisions imbued with the recognition that the road to peace is paved with sacrifices. His legacy, thus, not only illustrates the dualities of hope and despair but also signifies the complexities of navigating through ideologies and aspirations in pursuit of a greater good.

Ultimately, the compromises made in the lead-up to democracy offer crucial insights into the mechanisms of power, resistance, and leadership. Mandela's philosophical framework, grounded in love and reconciliation, helped to foster a democratic ethos rooted in pluralism. The reflections surrounding these compromises cast enduring lessons for future generations of leaders navigating the fragile terrains between ideology and pragmatism.

The political landscape of South Africa today still echoes the compromises that were made in those critical years. Mandela's leadership demonstrated that patience, dialogue, and a willingness to engage can foster environments for healing, even amidst immense resistance. The challenge remains for contemporary leaders to extract the teachings from this legacy, ensuring that the delicate balance between aspiration and reality does not dissolve into discord.

Voices of Discontent

In the wake of Nelson Mandela's ascendance to the presidency and the historic dismantling of apartheid, the African National Congress (ANC) celebrated a monumental victory. However, beneath the surface of this triumph lay an undercurrent of discontent that threatened to unravel the very fabric of the movement that had fought so valiantly for liberation. While Mandela was heralded as a beacon of hope for many, a growing chorus of voices emerged within the ANC and broader society, questioning the trajectory of the new government and the compromises that had been made during negotiations.

"Our human compassion binds us the one to the other — not in pity or patronizingly, but as human beings who have learnt how to turn our common suffering into hope for the future."

— Nelson Mandela

To fully comprehend this discontent, we must first examine the narratives from influential figures within the ANC who felt that Mandela's decisions post-negotiation veered towards betrayal of the revolution's principles. These voices, representing a wide spectrum of opinion, provided critical assessments of the political compromises that shaped the new South Africa.

As the transition from a liberation movement to a governing party solidified, many former activists felt an acute sense of loss regarding the revolutionary ideals that had fueled their struggle against apartheid. During a particularly poignant gathering of the ANC veterans in 1995, amid the celebratory atmosphere of the new democracy, a veteran leader, Zweli F. Nxumalo, voiced his feelings candidly. "We fought for liberation, but in that fight, we envisioned something radical, a system truly representative and liberatory for all," he said, "Now, I look around and see a government worried more about foreign investment than the basic needs of our people. Is this what we sacrificed so much for?"

Nxumalo's words echoed a sentiment prevalent among many ANC members who felt that the party's leadership, under Mandela's direction, had strayed too far from its roots. They feared that the compromises reached during negotiations with the apartheid government gave undue power to business interests and marginalized the poor, countryside communities that had long been the backbone of the ANC's support.

Beyond the ANC, South Africa's civil society began mobilizing discontent through various protests and activism, expressing dissatisfaction with unfulfilled promises. One of the most notable protests occurred in 1996, when thousands gathered outside the Parliament in Cape Town, brandishing placards that read, "Jobs and Housing Now!" and "People's Power!" This demonstration, organized by the Congress of South African Trade Unions (COSATU), represented a broader concern that the government, once filled with the hope of transformation, was prioritizing macroeconomic stability over basic social justice.

Amidst these tensions, critiques of the leadership began to emerge from an unlikely source—former comrades-in-arms who had fought alongside Mandela. In a series of interviews, Thabo Mbeki, who would later succeed Mandela, articulated the growing frustrations among party members. Mbeki pointedly remarked, "The ethos of urgent transformation that defined our past seems at odds with the reality of governance today. It's a delicate balance between pragmatism and idealism, and I worry we might be losing sight of the revolution we fought for."

Mbeki's transition from revolutionary to a government official exemplified the ambivalence many experienced during this period. The dual roles of being celebrated as a liberation hero while managing the complex apparatus of governance often led to moments of philosophical conflict. This disquiet within the ANC foreshadowed deeper rifts that would manifest later in South Africa's political landscape.

The rhetoric from grassroots organizations such as the Black Sash Federation was equally fervent. Founded during the anti-apartheid struggle, this women's organization passionately called for accountability and action on gender equity and economic justice. Their protests reflected the view that Mandela's administration was not doing enough to rectify the broader inequalities that persisted post-apartheid. Behind the clamor, members expressed a sentiment that the new government's neoliberal agendas were hindering progress for those who had suffered the most under apartheid's brutal regime.

In an open letter to Mandela published in the early 2000s, leading members of the Black Sash articulated their dismay: "As we have seen privatization and austerity measures enacted, we must ask ourselves, is our liberation merely the transfer of power from one elite to another? Are we not worthy of a government that prioritizes our needs and aspirations over corporate interests?"

These dissenting voices resonated not only within organized movements but also among ordinary citizens perplexed by the rapid changes occurring in their country. The experience of many South Africans who had expected immediate improvements in their lives revealed a stark gulf between people's expectations and the government's pace of reform. In a poignant interview, one community leader from a township summed up the frustrations of many when he stated, "We were told that the new government would bring jobs, housing, and dignity; instead, our lives remain the same, while the politicians seem more concerned with their international reputations."

The discontent transcended socio-economic lines, permeating through urban and rural communities alike. In the Eastern Cape, an area emblematic of the struggle for land rights, farmers and landless citizens protested against stalled agricultural reforms. Many within these communities expressed feelings of betrayal, asserting that the ANC had forgotten its roots in the rural struggles that marked the apartheid era.

A town hall meeting in a village near Mvezo, Mandela's birthplace, revealed intense local grievances. Here, community members expressed how expected land reforms had yet to materialize. An elder remarked, "Nelson Mandela may be our hero, but heroes can make mistakes, too. We waited for change and have not seen it. How can we trust the promises made?"

The ANC had become the custodian of political power, yet the gap between the party and the people grew more pronounced over the years, exacerbating the discontent felt by the very supporters who had risked their lives for liberation. The voices of dissent not only highlighted the inherent contradictions in the ANC's governance but also raised critical questions about the nature of leadership in a transitional society.

Protests continued to erupt with increasing regularity as the years passed. In 1998, the discontent culminated in a significant march led by activists dissatisfied with government policies—including issues of HIV/AIDS treatment access and pricing of essential services. One activist, Lucinda Mzazi, delivered a speech that would amplify the discourse on the expectations placed on leadership and the necessity for accountability. "We are not ungrateful for the freedom we have achieved. However, each day we face the reality of illness and poverty. This administration must address these issues because freedom is meaningless without a dignified existence."

Despite the growing unrest, Mandela continued to advocate for a message of unity and reconciliation, often reiterating that immediate, radical changes would not come without a measured approach to governance and reconciliation. His administration's commitment to reconciliation was seen as a necessary pillar to diffuse potential violence and division in a country grappling with its fraught history. However, this philosophy led some to believe that Mandela had become disconnected from the grassroots realities complicating the transformative struggle.

Critics from within called into question Mandela's prioritization of reconciliation over retribution. One vocal critic, ANC member and former combatant against apartheid, Andile Ndlovu, stated, "Reconciliation is important, but it cannot come at the expense of justice. We must address the grievances of our people; otherwise, we risk creating a gaping wound that will fester."

Mandela's dedication to maintaining a balanced approach eyed toward stability was continually challenged by those who felt reform came too slowly. This struggle encapsulated the broader paradox of his leadership: how to satisfy the revolutionary aspirations of the many while navigating the treacherous waters of governance.

> **"When the water starts boiling it is foolish to turn off the heat."**
>
> — Nelson Mandela

As a result, a schism began to widen between the older generation of ANC leaders and younger activists who felt a different sense of urgency. The emergence of the ANC Youth League as a more radical voice demanding swift and substantial changes illustrated this generational divide. They voiced sentiments that echoed throughout the movement's past, denouncing corruption, economic inequality, and compromised governance. "We fought for liberty, and we now demand equality," proclaimed a youth leader during a rally in 2000, underlining the prevailing sentiment among many that the revolution was unfinished.

The embrace of neoliberal economic policies under Mandela's presidency also generated significant dissent. Frustrations arose over budget allocations that targeted economic growth with little regard for addressing unemployment and poverty, evident in the critiques from trade unions and grassroots organizations alike. Statements from leaders like Zwelinzima Vavi, then-general secretary of the Congress of South African Trade Unions, articulated these grievances: "In pursuing a capitalist agenda, we are imperiling the very lives of those we once fought to free. We demand an agenda that places the worker at its center!"

With increasing public disapproval, the balance between social stability and the expectations of a transformative government became a constant theme within the ANC. Mandela's legacy was now being scrutinized through a harsh lens, assessing whether the compromises he made in the interests of the future had disenfranchised those who had fought for freedom alongside him.

The portrayal of leadership in this crucial epoch rendered Mandela's figure emblematic of the contradictions that plagued the transition from revolution to governance. How could a leader so revered be subjected to such scrutiny? This juxtaposition reflected the complex legacy of a man who had inspired millions but also became a target for criticism when the immediate fruits of liberation proved elusive.

As protests showcased increasing dissatisfaction, Mandela's place within the historical narrative was simultaneously cherished and challenged, painting a multifaceted picture of leadership in perilous times. The voices of dissent became an integral part of this narrative, illustrating not only the growing disconnect at the heart of the ANC but also the broader human cost of governance and the expectations of a nation striving to rebuild its identity.

In closing this chapter of discontent, it is essential to remember that the narratives of dissent do not negate the achievements of Mandela or the ANC; instead, they illuminate the complexities and contradictions inherent in transformative movements. The voices raised in protest were not merely criticisms; they represented hopes for a more just and equitable nation, reaffirming the responsibility not just to remember the revolution but to actively engage in its ongoing evolution.

Mandela's challenge, and that of future leaders, remains starkly relevant—a quest to embody the principles of liberation while navigating the exigencies of governance. The din of dissent serves as a clarion call for accountability, a reminder that true leadership must encompass the voices of all, particularly those still yearning for the reality of the dreams that once ignited the struggle for freedom.

Under the Microscope

In the discourse surrounding Nelson Mandela's leadership and the decisions he made during the transition from apartheid to a democratic South Africa, the complexities of his compromises cannot be overstated. The varied interpretations of his actions, viewed through scholarly and popular lenses, reveal a mosaic of understanding that illuminates different facets of his legacy. In this subchapter, we will critically analyze these interpretations, evaluate the implications of Mandela's compromises across various sectors, and synthesize critiques from political analysts, historians, and activists.

To begin, one must recognize that Mandela's approach was not solely reactive; it was a form of strategic pragmatism shaped by the harsh realities of the South African socio-political landscape. Even within the ANC, differing opinions on how to attain liberation created a profound rift in ideologies. According to historian Thula Simpson, the ANC faced a crucial dilemma.

"The leadership was caught between the idealism of the youth and the pragmatism of the elders who had seen the consequences of radical action. This created an atmosphere of tension where compromises were necessary for survival and progress."

On one hand, there were the radical elements within the ANC, who believed in a total overhaul of the system through robust confrontation. These factions, particularly within the ANC Youth League, espoused a militant approach that sought immediate and uncompromising reforms. They viewed Mandela's negotiation strategy as a dilution of the revolutionary spirit that had galvanized masses during years of oppression. Each compromise, therefore, came to be perceived as a step back from the revolutionary ideals that many young activists had grown to idolize.

Conversely, Mandela understood that for the ANC to transition into a ruling party, negotiating with adversaries was essential. Thus, his approach can be viewed as a balancing act that sought to unify conflicting ideologies within the ANC while addressing the demands of the apartheid government. Nelson Mandela biographer Anthony Sampson asserts, "Mandela recognized that sometimes, peace demands negotiation, and in those negotiations, hard choices must be made."

While the youth's fire for revolutionary change was evident, as articulated by the ANC Youth League leader, Julius Malema, who later formed the Economic Freedom Fighters, the call for direct action often clashed with Mandela's philosophy of reconciliation. Malema expressed criticism of Mandela's approach, stating, "We were ready to take back our land, seize banks, and transform this economy overnight. Our elders opted for discussions. They lost the spirit of the revolution."

The critiques surrounding Mandela's compromises often highlight specific instances, such as the insistence on retaining neoliberal economic policies, which some argue undermined the ANC's initial promise of land reform and socioeconomic equity. The impact of these policies cannot be overlooked, as prosperity largely remained within the hands of a white minority, hence fostering the perception that this new government was merely an extension of the previous apartheid regime with a different face.

The Economic Freedom Fighters have been particularly vocal against these policies, arguing that the compromises made during the negotiations effectively sustained economic inequalities and perpetuated a poverty cycle among black South Africans. In their view, Mandela chose to prioritize political stability over economic equity, an argument supported by numerous critics. In this context, political analyst Mcebisi Ndletyana states, "While Mandela was focused on creating a peaceful transition, the ideologies he adopted fitted neatly into a neoliberal framework that abandoned the radical goals of economic justice."

Furthermore, it is essential to assess the external pressures that Mandela faced throughout this negotiation process. Scholars like Richard Calland have argued that international actors—especially Western powers—played a significant role in shaping the terms of the transition. There was an overwhelming emphasis on maintaining stability and the status quo, which translated into a demand for compromises that sidelined radical policy changes.

"Countries will rally around any semblance of order, and the Western world at the time was not ready for any form of radical economic transformation that threatened their interests," Calland notes.

The implications of these external influences were profound and legitimized Mandela's decisions, which at times appeared to align more with the wishes of international actors than with the grassroots aspirations of ordinary South Africans. For instance, the negotiation processes reflected an acute awareness of global market dynamics, which stifled calls for deeper systemic changes. This insistence on free-market principles became a point of contention, raising various critiques that Mandela and his administration were simply upholding policies that benefitted the elite at the expense of the marginalized.

Nevertheless, some scholars argue that it would be unfair to label Mandela's decisions purely as a betrayal of the revolutionary spirit. Historical contexts and demands of the moment necessitated a level of compromise that often resulted in difficult, yet necessary, reconciliations. According to political scientist William Gumede, "Mandela understood that governance is not merely about achieving an end goal; it's about sustaining a society where coexistence is possible. It demanded that he make choices rooted in reality rather than idealism."

> **"A freedom fighter learns the hard way that it is the oppressor who defines the nature of the struggle."**
>
> — Nelson Mandela

While contrasting views abound, one must question whether Mandela's compromises resulted in a net positive or negative outcome for South Africa. A balanced analysis must extend beyond mere condemnation of his choices and seek to understand the multifaceted dynamics at play. Analyst Susan Booysen provides a nuanced critique, observing that Mandela, notwithstanding his compromises, invigorated a democratic process that facilitated vital dialogue among various factions within South African society.

"His compromises allowed diverse voices to be heard and facilitated dialogues that might otherwise have been impossible.

The political landscape became not just about confrontation but participation," she argues.

In evaluating the outcomes of Mandela's decisions, it is also crucial to consider the pivotal role of reconciliation and nation-building, embodied in initiatives like the Truth and Reconciliation Commission (TRC). While some regarded the TRC as insufficient, compromising on the pursuit of justice in favor of societal stability, others saw it as a necessary step towards healing a fractured nation. The TRC enabled victims to voice their experiences, bringing forth narratives that were imperative for rebuilding national identity.

Mandela's acknowledgment of the strengths and vulnerabilities within human nature influenced his decision to incorporate restorative justice rather than punitive measures. The TRC, as historian Mahmood Mamdani argues, was revolutionary in its framing of a society that sought healing without demonization. "It was a departure from a retribution-centered justice, aiming instead to spotlight the truth of all experiences, therefore highlighting the need for common humanity in the face of historical wrongs."

However, the TRC also raised concerns about its efficacy in addressing accountability, with countless victims lamenting that the perpetrators of violence had faced minimal consequences for their actions. Activist groups like Khulumani Support Group argued that the TRC's failures to deliver justice reflected the very compromises Mandela engaged in. Critics within these circles suggest that the evasion of stringent accountability measures contributed to the pervasive social injustices witnessed in post-apartheid South Africa. The effects of these compromises extended to perceptions of legitimacy concerning the ANC's governance, particularly amongst the youth who felt increasingly abandoned by a party that failed to address their socio-economic aspirations.

In the same vein, the economic compromises betrayed a generation of South Africans who had pinned their hopes on the promise of a liberated society that fundamentally addressed historical inequalities. The failure to enact radical economic reforms became a defining feature of Mandela's legacy, wherein political centers of power were contrasted against the socio-economic struggles that persisted. Activist and scholar Andile Mngxitama emphasizes the need to confront these realities, stating, "Compromise in politics can often translate into betrayal for those whose hunger for freedom extends beyond political representation and into the very essence of their livelihoods."

As such, echoes of discontent will inevitably resonate within the collective psyche of the nation. As the years passed, subsequent ANC administrations were met with noise not only from within but also from disenfranchised communities. Public protests reflected a disillusioned populace grappling with the disconnect between their expectations and lived realities.

In summary, as we put Nelson Mandela's compromises under the microscope, it becomes clear that these decisions garner divergent evaluations reflective of broader, unresolved tensions about leadership, justice, and radical change. Critics may emphasize the compromises as failures of revolutionary promises to enact structural change. Conversely, proponents draw attention to the pragmatic necessity of creating a stable foundation amidst volatile circumstances. It is this complexity that continues to evoke intense conversations about what it means to lead a revolution in a multifaceted world. Each critique serves as a lens through which to view the layered consequences of Mandela's choices.

Understanding Mandela's legacy, therefore, requires engaging with this spectrum of interpretations, for Mandela was both a product of his time and a visionary grappling with the burdens of leadership. In the aftermath of apartheid, a nation forged in compromise must still reckon with the dissonance created by the ideals of liberation juxtaposed against the compromises made in its name. The inquiry into Mandela's decisions extends beyond mere leadership analysis, pushing us towards deeper reflections on justice, identity, and the economics that define the lives of millions in contemporary South Africa.

Understanding Legacy

In the realms of history and leadership, the concept of legacy is a weighty one, echoing through time and influencing generations long after the leaders themselves have passed. For Nelson Mandela, a man hailed as a beacon of hope and a fighter for justice, this notion takes on a profound complexity, particularly in the context of the choices he made during his presidency and the broader narrative of the African National Congress (ANC). To understand Mandela's legacy is to engage in a philosophical discourse that examines not only his achievements as a leader but the nuanced balance he sought between idealism and pragmatism amid the tumultuous landscape of post-apartheid South Africa.

Legacy does not exist in a vacuum; it is the product of choices made, sacrifices endured, and the collective memories of a people. For Mandela, the choices he made, especially those perceived as compromises, haunt discussions about his legacy. The monumental choice to negotiate with a regime that had long oppressed his people rather than pursue a more radical confrontation is a focal point of this inquiry. Did he betray the revolution, or did he demonstrate a profound understanding of the forces at play within the political landscape? In answering these questions, one must grapple with how leaders define their legacies through their actions and the principles that guide them.

Mandela's journey illustrates a delicate dance between idealism—the belief in the possibility of a just society free from the chains of oppression—and pragmatism, which often necessitates difficult decisions that can undermine ideological purity. He entered the political arena as a firebrand, his spirit ignited by the injustices surrounding him. He envisioned a South Africa where every citizen enjoyed equal rights and freedom, where the scars of apartheid could be healed through unity and reconciliation. Yet, as he transitioned from a radical young leader to the president of a nation in flux, his vision had to contend with a new reality—one riddled with complexities and the expectations of countless stakeholders.

The legacy of Nelson Mandela is intricately tied to his strategies of balancing these sometimes conflicting ideals. He recognized that the road to liberation was not merely about overthrowing an oppressive regime but also about constructing a cohesive and workable political framework in its aftermath. In this balancing act, Mandela exemplified what many call transformative leadership. He understood that to be an effective leader, one must navigate the turbulent waters of social expectations, political realities, and personal convictions.

This philosophical exploration of leadership in the face of monumental choices invites us to question what true leadership entails. Is it simply about achieving lofty ideals, or is it about the willingness to compromise for greater good? Mandela embodied both perspectives. His commitment to reconciliation and negotiation with the apartheid government transformed not only the political landscape of South Africa but also redefined the very nature of leadership. The ideals of freedom, equality, and justice became the foundation upon which he built his legacy, but they were often tempered with necessity—the need to forge a new path for a nation steeped in division.

Critics of Mandela often cite his compromises with the apartheid government as evidence of betrayal. They argue that by choosing to negotiate with adversaries and sacrificing certain revolutionary principles, he paved the way for a political environment that may have eroded the ANC's foundational tenets. Yet, it is essential to approach such critiques with a lens that appreciates the broader context. The alternative to his negotiation could have led to an even more profound turmoil, potentially plunging the nation back into cycles of violence and instability.

> "Reconciliation does not mean forgetting or trying to bury the pain of conflict, but that reconciliation means working together to correct the legacy of past injustice."
>
> — Nelson Mandela

The complexity of Mandela's decisions highlights the often-uncomfortable truth that idealism alone cannot sustain a revolution; pragmatism must step in. The South African context required a deft leader who understood the delicate balance between maintaining a revolutionary spirit while also addressing the stark realities of governance. Mandela's willingness to engage with those who oppressed him—transforming foes into partners—demonstrates leadership that prioritizes the greater good over personal or ideological purity.

He approached each decision with the understanding that his legacy would be evaluated not merely on the basis of his aspirations for the future but also on how he navigated the present's challenges. This approach manifests in the establishment of the Truth and Reconciliation Commission (TRC), a platform that exemplified his commitment to healing a divided nation. The TRC sought to acknowledge past atrocities while fostering a dialogue aimed at reconciliation, showcasing Mandela's understanding that justice, in its truest sense, requires more than retribution.

In distinguishing between betrayal and balance, one must appreciate that the legacy Mandela left behind was not merely a product of his policies or political decisions but a reflection of his character as a leader. He embodied the spirit of ubuntu, an African philosophy emphasizing communal interdependence and humanity. This foundational belief guided him to prioritize community over individual ambition and harmonized his idealism with the pragmatic demands of his role as a president. The legacy he crafted stands as a testament to the intricate relationship between aspiration and reality.

Moreover, Mandela's legacy challenges contemporary leaders to rethink the paradigms of leadership today. In a world often characterized by polarization and divisive rhetoric, his example beckons leaders to seek unity and understanding, even among adversaries. It encourages a re-examination of the sometimes rigid distinctions between enemies and allies, understanding that collaboration can yield transformative results—the very essence of revolutionary change.

As leaders grapple with monumental choices in their own contexts—a challenge not unique to Mandela—the principles embedded in his legacy resonate. His navigation of complex political landscapes implies that a leader's success is not solely measured by adherence to theory or ideology but also by the effectiveness with which they respond to the needs of those they serve. Mandela's legacy illustrates that the heart of leadership lies in the willingness to adapt, to listen, and to act with compassion and foresight.

This legacy of understanding and compromise is perhaps most pronounced in today's discourse surrounding governance, justice, and equality. The reverberation of Mandela's ideals can be found in movements advocating for social justice worldwide, echoing the belief that leadership requires both passion and pragmatism. Leaders are now tasked with navigating their societies not only with the ambition of achieving ideals but also with an acute awareness that history is watching—and that legacy will be determined by how effectively they forge paths forward in communities often fraught with divisions.

Ultimately, understanding legacy through the lens of leadership calls for a reflective consideration of the choices made in the pursuit of justice and equality. In Mandela's case, this reflection is enriched by a deep sense of empathy and an enduring commitment to building a better future. As we explore the complexities of his legacy, we are confronted with the imperative to recognize that true leadership transcends the mythic ideal; it is tethered to the authentic choices made in the face of adversity.

In contemplating Mandela's legacy, we are presented with the example of a leader who walked the tightrope between ambition and reality, never losing sight of the broader vision that guided him. His ability to understand the delicate balance between revolutionary zeal and the cautious strategies required to govern in an inherently divided society provides a roadmap for contemporary leaders. It implores them to embrace a holistic vision of leadership, one that remains grounded in the ideals of justice, equality, and human dignity.

As we reflect on these themes, we must articulate our aspirations for leadership in a world characterized by its complexities. Mandela's synthesis of idealism and pragmatism serves as a critical reminder that the legacies we leave behind will tell stories not simply of victories or defeats but of the choices we made along the way. The indelible mark of Mandela's legacy challenges us to aspire towards a leadership that embodies compassion, seeks understanding across divides, and recognizes that enduring change is often the result of compromise and negotiation.

In conclusion, understanding legacy through the complexities of a leader's choices fosters a more nuanced view of historical narratives. Mandela's journey teaches us that the art of leadership requires navigating difficult waters while keeping the ultimate goal of liberation and justice at the forefront of our aspirations. His legacy is a call to balance our convictions with the realities we face, reminding us that each decision made can ripple through time, shaping the future, and impacting the lives of generations yet to come. The essence of Mandela's legacy is not merely that he was a freedom fighter or a president; it is that he exemplified the profound impact of leadership grounded in empathy, adaptability, and a steadfast commitment to the principles of human dignity and justice.

The ANC's Resurgence

"A good head and a good heart are
always a formidable combination."

– Nelson Mandela

Internal Dynamics at Play

In the wake of Nelson Mandela's historic presidency, the African National Congress (ANC) found itself navigating uncharted waters, plagued by an intricate web of internal dynamics that would shape its identity and influence in the years to come. The transition from a liberation movement to a governing party came with profound challenges, as the leadership grappled with diverging ideologies, power struggles, and the expectations of a multifaceted electorate. This period was not merely an extension of Mandela's legacy; rather, it constituted a critical juncture that prompted both introspection and conflict within the ANC.

Mandela's presidency had been heralded as a triumph of reconciliation and unity, but the reality of governance proved to be far more complex. The ANC had long been driven by a singular goal: the dismantling of apartheid and the establishment of a democratic South Africa. However, once in power, a plethora of issues arose that demanded immediate attention, from economic inequalities to intra-party dissent.

As the ANC transitioned to governance, varying factions began to emerge, each with distinct agendas and visions for the future of South Africa. Key figures who had played critical roles during the anti-apartheid struggle found themselves at odds over the direction of the party and the nation.

> **"Lead from the back — and let others believe they are in front."**
>
> — Nelson Mandela

Among the prominent leaders were Thabo Mbeki, who succeeded Mandela as president, and Jacob Zuma, the Secretary-General of the ANC. Mbeki, an intellectual with a vision for an economically robust South Africa, advocated for neoliberal policies aimed at attracting foreign investment and fostering growth. His focus on macroeconomic stability often clashed with the grassroots aspirations of the party base, which called for a more radical departure from the injustices of apartheid, including land reform and wealth redistribution.

Conversely, Jacob Zuma emerged as a champion of the more populist sentiments within the party. He drew significant support from the labor unions and lower-income communities. His tenure as Deputy President was marked by alliances with influential factions within the ANC, particularly the South African Communist Party and the Congress of South African Trade Unions (COSATU). These alliances signaled a shift towards a more radical, leftist approach to governance, appealing to those who felt left behind in the post-apartheid era.

The ideological rift between Mbeki and Zuma was symptomatic of broader tensions within the ANC. Mbeki's administration was often perceived as elitist, deeply engaged in international diplomacy and economic strategies that, while advancing certain sectors, alienated many of the grassroots supporters. His focus on macroeconomic policies like the Growth, Employment and Redistribution strategy, while theoretically sound, did little to alleviate the acute poverty that persisted in black communities. The growing discontent among these constituents laid fertile ground for Zuma's rise, as he resonated with the narrative of struggle against inequality.

The ANC's internal conflicts would soon become more than mere ideological disagreements. In a party that had prided itself on its unity and singularity of purpose during the anti-apartheid struggle, the burgeoning rivalries sparked significant power struggles. Accusations of corruption, nepotism, and infighting plagued Mbeki's presidency, culminating in his eventual recall from the presidency in 2008. This internal strife highlighted vulnerabilities within the ANC, as rivals seized upon perceived weaknesses to challenge established leaders and vie for power.

The emergence of factions such as the so-called "Zuma camp" effectively polarized the party. This division was not merely about personalities; it revolved around deeply rooted differences in political philosophy and strategy. While the Mbeki camp focused on economic growth through globalization and privatization, the Zuma camp prioritized the reassertion of state power to fulfill the socio-economic demands of the populace. Each faction cemented its influence through strategic alliances and criticisms of the opposing camp, leading to an increasingly fractious political landscape within the ANC.

The personal stakes were high, with power within the party translating into access to resources and political patronage. The control of various ANC structures became a battleground, as supporters of each faction leveraged party support for their respective leaders. Loyalty was often tested, and political maneuvering assumed center stage.

As 2009 approached, South Africa became a focal point of scrutiny as the country prepared for a new election cycle. Jacob Zuma ascended to the presidency, a process marked by intense negotiations and strategic alliances formed during the years leading up to the polls. His election was seen by many as a rejection of Mbeki's policies and an embrace of a more radical approach to governance. However, Zuma's presidency also unleashed another wave of tensions, as he became embroiled in a series of corruption scandals that threatened to eclipse his leadership.

The internal dynamics within the ANC continued to evolve in the years that followed, as various factions jockeyed for position and influence. Zuma's presidency, characterized by allegations of state capture and mismanagement, brought to the surface long-standing grievances among party members disillusioned with what they perceived as a betrayal of the ANC's foundational principles. The growing discontent culminated in the rise of the Economic Freedom

Fighters (EFF), a newly formed party espousing radical leftist ideals, and positioning itself as a voice for those disillusioned by the ANC's failure to deliver meaningful economic transformation.

Zuma's presidency marked a turning point where the ideological battle lines were drawn clearly across the ANC. The growing rifts were exacerbated by the formation of coalitions and alliances outside of traditional ANC structures, reflecting an urgent need for change that transcended party politics. Figures like Julius Malema, formerly of the ANC Youth League, harnessed the rhetoric of discontent to call for an immediate shift in socio-economic policies, focusing on land restitution and wealth redistribution.

The ideological battles within the ANC also coincided with broader societal changes. As discontent grew among ordinary South Africans over socio-economic issues such as unemployment, service delivery, and corruption, the ANC faced a critical juncture in how it would navigate these challenges. The party's historical legacy was constantly under public scrutiny, as citizens questioned whether the very tenets of liberation had been eroded in the face of modern governance.

The tension within the ANC was not just confined to its leaders; it permeated through the organization's structures, leaving branches and constituencies at odds with one another. Grassroots supporters began expressing their dissatisfaction openly, staging protests and demanding accountability from their leaders. The ANC, once a symbol of hope and liberation, faced growing fears of losing its relevance as a political force. Factions began to splinter further, indicating a disconnect between the ANC's leadership and the aspirations of its base.

While Mandela's legacy was one of reconciliation, the post-Mandela years frequently witnessed calls for accountability and transparency, with criticisms mounting against leadership style and direction. Imbued with Mandela's spirit of activism, the party base showed an unwillingness to remain passive as events unraveled within the ANC. The reality was that the ANC was grappling with questions of representation and integrity, ultimately reflecting the challenges faced by emerging democracies worldwide.

As the dust settled in the aftermath of Zuma's scandal-ridden presidency, it became clear that the internal dynamics of the ANC continued to shape not only the party but South Africa as a whole. Following his removal from power, Cyril Ramaphosa was elected as president of the ANC and, subsequently, the country. His leadership represented yet another chapter in the ongoing struggle for the soul of the party, as he sought to steer a course toward rebuilding trust and restoring faith among both party members and the public.

Ramaphosa's tenure introduced a renewed focus on anti-corruption measures and economic reforms aimed at revitalizing the party's image. Such initiatives were met with mixed reactions, as the internal factions remained deeply entrenched in opposing visions for governance. The ideological schisms continued to pose challenges, requiring delicate negotiation among various party quarters to ensure a semblance of unity.

In conclusion, the internal dynamics at play within the ANC after Mandela's presidency encapsulated a broader struggle within post-apartheid South Africa. As the party navigated the complexities of governance, it found itself in the throes of ideological conflicts and power struggles that would ultimately define its trajectory in the coming years. Key figures emerged with competing visions, reflecting wider societal tensions and unmet aspirations. This rich tapestry of dissent and conflict not only highlights the challenges of managing change within a revolutionary movement but also raises critical questions about the capacity for unity and accountability in a post-liberation era. The legacy of Mandela may continue to inspire, but the road to realization remains fraught with obstacles that demand introspection, resilience, and a recommitment to the tenets of equality and justice that initially ignited the movement.

Reflections of a Nation

The post-apartheid era in South Africa, heralded by the transition from decades of oppressive rule to a multi-racial democracy, remains a vibrant tapestry of hopes, ideals, struggles, and disappointments. At the heart of this transformation lies Nelson Mandela, whose presidency symbolizes both a pinnacle of progress and a complex journey fraught with unmet aspirations. As South Africans reflected upon Mandela's impact, their thoughts revealed a kaleidoscope of emotions ranging from elation to disenchantment.

This subchapter endeavors to capture these reflections—a narrative rich in personal accounts, collective memories, and the systemic realities shaping the nation's perception of its beloved leader.

Mandela's ascent to the presidency in 1994 marked a watershed moment not only for himself but for an entire nation eager for change. Citizens rejoiced as they cast their ballots for the first time, eschewing years of subjugation under apartheid. Streets thrummed with celebration; the air was alive with songs of victory as people danced, waved flags, and held aloft the portraits of their long-imprisoned hero. The ideals Mandela embodied—freedom, reconciliation, and unity—resonated deeply within a populace yearning for a brighter future. In those moments, the nation felt invincible, bound together by a common dream of democracy.

Yet, as time progressed, the euphoria that accompanied his ascendency would be tempered by the complexities of governing a nation fragmented by years of division. The initial hopes burgeoned into expectations—expectations that were often met with stark realities. South Africans, from the bustling streets of Johannesburg to the rural landscapes of the Eastern Cape, began to grapple with the nuances of transformation, reflecting on the profound impacts of Mandela's policies as they navigated their daily lives.

Citizens spoke about Mandela's emphasis on reconciliation—how he urged forgiveness rather than punishment, fostering a spirit of unity that transcended racial divides. Nelson Mandela's charisma and his ability to connect with the hearts of ordinary people offered solace to many who had endured the injustices of apartheid. His focus on nation-building inspired a belief in peace over conflict, a beacon of hope that ignited the spirit of reconciliation in a society thought to be irreparably fractured.

Stories from individuals resonate throughout the narrative of Mandela's presidency, illustrating how countless South Africans rallied behind his vision. A township resident recalled joyously voting in 1994 and felt a sense of dignity for the first time in her life. "Mandela gave us hope," she declared with a sense of pride. Such sentiments echoed across communities, as many found strength in the ideal that South Africa could emerge from the darkness of its past to become a beacon of peace and prosperity.

However, beneath the surface of hope lay unresolved frustrations. As years passed, citizens began to feel that the anticipated dividends of democracy were not reaching them rapidly enough. The profound socio-economic disparities that characterized the apartheid era hadn't dissipated; instead, they had morphed in insidious ways, reconnecting the past with the present through persistent inequalities. A mother in the rural village of Tzaneen lamented, "We thought Mandela would bring us jobs, opportunities. Instead, my children still struggle to find work, even with degrees." Such candid reflections reveal the chasm that grew between public expectations and political deliverables.

Corruption, inefficiency, and allegations of cronyism began to cloud the perception of the ANC itself, the very institution Mandela had revitalized. While he stood as a paragon of integrity, others within the party were implicated in scandals that marred the collective image of a party that had once fought valiantly for liberation. Public sentiment began to shift; disillusionment blended with nostalgia for the simpler hope of the early 90s. At community meetings, residents voiced concerns: "What happened to the values they promised us?" echoed the words of many in local assemblies, searching for accountability from leaders in whom they had once placed unwavering faith.

> "The brave man is not he who does not feel afraid, but he who conquers that fear."
>
> — Nelson Mandela

Mandela's successors, while inspired by his vision, struggled to fulfill the promises made during the fervent days of the revolution. This dissonance manifested in the broader socio-political landscape. Citizens aired their grievances, often contrasting the high ideals of Mandela's presidency with the lax governance of subsequent leaders. As protests erupted across the country in response to service delivery failures, the legacy of struggle became a canvas splattered with frustration that contrasted sharply with the ideals Mandela had set forth. In informal settlements, residents echoed their dissatisfaction:

"We are still living in shacks; they say we are free, but what kind of freedom is this?"

The disquieting sense of responsibility for the transformation of the nation weighed heavily on Mandela's shoulders. As he witnessed the gradual decline in public trust toward the ANC, he remained a figure who called for unity and perseverance. In his speeches, he implored his fellow countrymen to stay true to the principles of equality and justice, urging them to work towards the ideals they once fought so fervently to attain. Yet, many citizens felt that the complexities of daily governance and the demands of political reality had shoved those cherished ideals aside.

As the nation grappled with its realities, the reflections on Mandela's legacy are invariably tied to the themes of hope and disappointment. In many discussions, one can find an oscillation between idealism and realism, as citizens confront the multi-layered dimensions of freedom. While the symbolic power of Mandela's presidency continues to resonate within the consciousness of the nation, the quest for a complete realization of that vision is marred by the infrastructural, economic, and social challenges that persist.

Furthermore, the emergence of a new generation, one that grew up post-apartheid, adds another layer of complexity to the reflections on Mandela's legacy. Young South Africans express admiration for his contributions but voice frustration over the pacing of change—"We have our rights, but they don't translate into opportunities," lamented a student at the University of Cape Town. This statement embodies the growing sentiment of impatience, particularly among youth who look at the successes of the revolution and demand that their leaders deliver meaningful change to ensure their futures.

Diversity of thought regarding Mandela's presidency highlights the need for a multifaceted understanding of legacy. Reflections from women in various sectors illustrate how gendered perspectives emerge as crucial lenses through which the past is viewed. For many women, Mandela represented not only a liberator from racial oppression but also a catalyst for gender rights. They often encompass both gratitude and frustration, citing Mandela's commitment to equality while acknowledging that societal and structural feminism continues to lag painfully behind. A women's group participant remarked, "Mandela celebrated us, but the fight for our rights is far from over." Hence, the legacy reflects resilient yet unresolved aspirations across multifarious communities.

In terms of economic reforms, sentiments oscillate between pride in the progress made and distress over the uneven distribution of resources. The Freedom Charter's promises of equitable economic engagement seem largely unfulfilled, as inequality persists despite the overarching narrative of progress. Migrant workers narrate their tales of hardship and resilience; they contribute to national growth yet find themselves on the fringes of economic opportunity. "We came for a better future but often find only disappointment," shared a laborer in a local workshop, capturing the experiences of many who felt abandoned in the aftermath of transformation.

In evaluating public opinion, it becomes clear that Mandela transcended mere political office and emerged as an enduring symbol of perseverance and hope. His ability to navigate a reconciliatory path, while calling for accountability from those in power, remains enshrined in the public psyche.

Yet, this narrative is not without its conflicts. Mandela's decisions—sometimes viewed through a transformative lens—are scrutinized for their outcomes. Questions loom: Did his choices pave the way for sustainable governance, or did they sow the seeds of a cycle of disappointment? As citizens ponder these questions, the need for an inclusive discourse surrounding Mandela's impact remains crucial for the nation's healing and growth.

Public sentiment thus weaves a narrative of complex intertwining stories—a nation in transition, grappling with the ideals of its revolutionary past while forging its future. Collective memories, imbued with layers of emotional resonance, anchor the discussion of Mandela's presidency in both triumph and disappointment. As South Africa continues to navigate its path, the reflections on Mandela, the cherished leader, will remain dynamic—reflecting hope, resilience, and the enduring struggle for a more equitable society.

The reflections of this nation, as caught through the voices of its citizens, reveal the enduring power of Mandela's legacy. While Mandela's era might have passed, the legacy of his aspirations persists through the hopes and challenges of South Africa today. In capturing these reflections, one is left with a profound understanding that the journey is ongoing—a quest for identity, purpose, and unity that underpins the heart of post-apartheid South Africa.

Ultimately, the narrative evolved from celebration to introspection, securing Mandela's place not only in history but in the collective consciousness of South Africans who continue striving for a home where freedom and equality are not just promises but tangible realities. As citizens engage in ongoing conversations surrounding justice, integrity, and hope, they find that Mandela's vision continues to guide them, illuminating the path toward a brighter future—a reflection of enduring hope amidst an ever-evolving reality.

Crisis of Identity

In the euphoria following the end of apartheid, the African National Congress (ANC) emerged as a victorious liberation movement, basking in the sentiments of a nation eager for transformation and unity. However, as the ANC transitioned into a governing party, it faced an identity crisis that threatened its foundational principles. The distance between revolutionary ideals and the pragmatic reality of governance widened, leading to internal conflicts and public disillusionment. This subchapter delves into the complexities of this crisis of identity, exploring how the ANC grappled with its historical legacy while trying to align itself with the demands of governance in a democratic South Africa.

The ANC's struggle against apartheid was characterized by unwavering commitment to justice, freedom, and equality—a struggle that galvanized millions both within South Africa and across the globe. The party's deep roots in the anti-apartheid movement defined its identity: it was the embodiment of the fight for liberation, often marked by sacrifices from its leaders and operatives. Iconic struggles and profound narratives of resistance cultivated a culture of idealism intertwined with nationalism, reverberating with the voices of a people yearning for dignity and justice.

Yet, the victory claimed in 1994 came with unforeseen challenges. The ANC's transition to governance required a shift not just in its operational strategies but also in its very essence. The party had to navigate the demands of political power while attempting to remain true to its revolutionary ideals. This was a delicate balancing act that sparked discomfort and apprehension within its ranks, where veterans of the struggle met younger, politically savvy professionals eager to shape a government that functioned efficiently.

The ANC's primary challenge lay in reconciling its revolutionary past with the expectations of a contemporary democratic government—an entity that is often viewed through a pragmatic lens of accountability, efficiency, and results. As the new government sought to implement policies aimed at redressing past injustices, the foundational principles of the ANC were tested. How could the party maintain its commitment to social justice while also addressing the bureaucratic needs of a state?

The dynamics within the ANC showcased a profound ideological struggle. Prominent figures within the party debated the relevance of revolutionary rhetoric in a time of governance. Some insisted on preserving the resolute, uncompromising spirit of the liberation struggle while others argued for a shift towards a governance model driven by realism and strategic alliances—ideas often perceived as a betrayal of the movement's ideals.

Internal disagreements sparked tensions among members, especially as the socio-economic situation in South Africa remained grim. Critically high unemployment rates and deepening poverty levels posed serious questions about the efficacy of ANC policies. The vast gulf between its manifesto rhetoric and the lived experiences of many South Africans led to rising dissatisfaction among the electorate. Disenchantment surfaced through protests, strikes, and public calls for greater accountability, often directed at the ruling party's ability to fulfill its promises of a better life for all.

Public sentiment began to shift. Many South Africans, particularly those who were not part of the elite inner circles, felt their voices were being stifled. The ANC had once been a beacon of hope, representing the oppressed, yet as leaders took up positions of authority, a prevailing narrative emerged: the party was becoming increasingly disconnected from the people's struggles. The contradiction of being both liberators and rulers proved challenging, as citizens demanded transparency and tangible outcomes in their daily lives while grappling with the complexities introduced by governance.

As internal and external pressures mounted, the ANC found itself at an ideological crossroads. Key debates centered on issues such as economic redistributive justice versus the need for fiscal responsibility. ANC leaders wrestled with the cognition that their decisions could either bolster or betray the historic revolutionary ethos, leading to considerable dissent within the party's ranks. The voices of the youth began to rise—those who had grown up in a post-apartheid South Africa and were increasingly impatient with the slow pace of change. This generational rift posed a significant challenge, as the old guard sought to clench onto the legacy of the past, yet the youth demanded an evolution that spoke to contemporary needs and aspirations.

Moreover, facing the realities of governance required the ANC to engage with various factions—including business leaders, traditional leaders, and international financiers—who often had conflicting interests. The pursuit of economic growth and foreign investment sometimes clashed with the ideals of radical economic transformation and land reform that were central to the ANC's mission. Navigating these contrasting priorities manifested in two distinct camps within the ANC: those advocating for an adherence to leftist ideologies and those pushing for neo-liberal economic policies.

The growth of corruption and scandals within the party further compounded the crisis of identity. Allegations concerning the misuse of power, patronage, and a growing culture of entitlement sent shockwaves through the ranks of idealistic supporters. As the ANC grappled with these issues, a sense of betrayal—particularly among the very constituencies that had fought tirelessly for freedom—loomed large. The ideals of the liberation struggle seemed to fracture as egregious missteps overshadowed the party's original vision.

Public figures, activists, and even long-time supporters began to openly question whether the ANC was still defending the cause it once championed. Examples of disenchantment are plentiful—from the creation of alternative political movements to the massive protests fueled by the dissatisfaction with ANC governance. Each protest, each movement symbolized a growing concern: had the ANC sacrificed its identity on the altar of political expediency?

> **"No country can really develop unless its citizens are educated."**
>
> — Nelson Mandela

The response from leadership was mixed. While some ANC members sought to reaffirm the party's core revolutionary ideals amid the noise of dissent, others opted for pragmatism, believing it necessary for survival in a rapidly changing political environment. As a result, a new narrative started to emerge, one that attempted to encapsulate the complexities of governance while drawing from the ethos of the struggle.

Efforts to rehabilitate the party's image involved invoking the language of unity and solidarity—campaigns emphasizing continued dedication to upliftment, empowerment, and equality. Yet, even as such rhetoric could resonate with voters, the gap between speech and action proved increasingly vast. South Africans scrutinized whether the ANC was equipped to prioritize moral governance or if it would fall prey to the temptations of power.

Simultaneously, the ANC's historical legacy became a double-edged sword. The valiant struggles against apartheid conjured national pride, yet they also carried the weight of expectation. How could the party's leadership honor the legacy of past sacrifices while effectively responding to the demands of modern governance?

As the party moved deeper into its governance role, the juxtaposition of the ANC's role as a revolutionary body versus that of a ruling entity fostered debates regarding salvation and failure. Political analysts, historians, and citizens alike began framing the legitimacy of the ANC through the lens of its ability to deliver outcomes. The party's trajectory became the subject of ardent discussions, with critics challenging whether the ANC represented an evolving state entity or was now merely an establishment concerned with maintaining power at all costs.

The notion of identity became critical during this turbulent phase. Questions of what it meant to be an ANC member morphed into broader discussions about what it meant to be a South African after apartheid. In this newly defined landscape, many began exploring the concept of a post-ANC identity, piquing interests in alternative visions for governance and representation that diverged from the ANC's historical grip. The discontent echoed broadly, as citizens deliberated if they could entrust their futures to a party that had become synonymous with both liberation and, increasingly, perceived failure.

In response to the challenges it faced, the ANC began acknowledging the need for introspection and reevaluation of its identity. Public speeches emphasized the importance of renewal, accountability, and reconnecting with the grassroots. Initiatives surfaced within party ranks seeking to return to community engagements, striving to re-establish a bond with constituents that had begun to fray amid the struggles for power and influence. Some leaders introduced measures aimed at improving transparency, but the specter of past governance failures lingered heavily.

Yet, for many within the ANC, these initiatives often felt like an insufficient response to a deep-seated crisis. The call for political rejuvenation resonated amidst generational divides, prompting discourse about whether the ANC could recalibrate itself without relinquishing its historical essence. As a result, the responses from different factions within the party varied in their commitment to bridging the identity gap.

The calls for transformation within the ANC represented a mix of nostalgia for the past and hope for future possibilities. Contextualizing self-critique and recognition of shortcomings became essential for survival, granting the audience an opportunity to witness an evolution within the ANC. Activists, community leaders, and even younger political figures remained ever aware of the need for a party that would translate revolutionary fervor into tangible outcomes.

As the ANC continued to wrestle with its identity crisis, the political landscape shifted further. Emerging parties captured segments of the electorate disillusioned by ANC policies that had failed to fulfill their aspirations. This landscape prompted deep reflection on the necessity of integrating revolutionary ideals with the realities of governance, and a renewed sense of purpose—one grounded in the urgency of the present and the complexities that lay ahead.

Ultimately, the ANC's identity crisis presents a multifaceted narrative laden with tensions between legacy and reform. As the party navigates the intricacies of its historical positioning while seeking to find its footing in contemporary governance, its journey reflects broader themes relevant to any movement undergoing significant transformations. The balance between maintaining high-minded ideals and addressing pressing realities becomes crucial as South Africa moves forward.

In examining the identity crisis within the ANC, it becomes clear that navigating the fraught terrain between the ambitions of a liberation movement and the responsibilities of governing is inherently challenging. The ANC stands as a testament to this struggle, as it endeavors to redefine its identity amid the specter of its past, while charting a path that aligns with the hopes of future generations.

Legacy
in the Lattice

*"What counts in life is not the mere fact
that we have lived. It is what difference we
have made to the lives of others that will
determine the significance of the life we lead."*

— Nelson Mandela

A Society in Transition

In the aftermath of apartheid, South Africa emerged into a new era filled with opportunities and challenges. The transition from a segregated past to a unified nation was fraught with complexities that impacted every aspect of society. While Nelson Mandela's leadership paved the way for democracy and reconciliation, the realities of post-apartheid South Africa revealed deep-seated social issues and economic disparities that continued to affect millions of citizens.

The first crucial area to examine is the social fabric of South Africa post-1994. Despite the formal abolition of apartheid, the lingering effects of decades of institutionalized racism were embedded within communities. The transition was not merely a political shift but a fundamental change in societal dynamics. Mandela and the ANC envisioned a society where all citizens, regardless of race, would have equal access to opportunities. Nevertheless, the social landscape was marked by profound inequalities that were not easily dismantled overnight.

> **"No one is born hating another person because of the color of his skin, or his background, or his religion."**
>
> — Nelson Mandela

Housing conditions illustrated the stark contrast between the ideals of a new democracy and the harsh reality faced by many. The influx of people into urban areas in search of jobs exacerbated the housing crisis. Townships, often located on the peripheries of cities, were overcrowded, under-resourced, and plagued by lack of infrastructure. Although Mandela's government made significant strides in housing development, including the construction of affordable homes, the pace of progress often lagged behind the need. Many South Africans did not have access to basic services such as clean water, sanitation, and electricity, leading to heightened frustrations and a sense of betrayal among communities that had placed their hopes in a new regime.

Education was another critical area where South Africa struggled to reconcile the past with the present. While the new government pledged to provide quality education for all, disparities in schooling reflected the deep divisions left by apartheid. Schools in impoverished areas were underfunded and overcrowded, lacking the resources necessary to deliver quality education. In contrast, previously privileged schools continued to thrive, creating a chasm between the educational experiences of different racial groups. Mandela's commitment to education as a driver of change was clear, yet the reality was that many children were still trapped in a failing system. The disparities in education perpetuated cycles of poverty and contributed to youth disillusionment, as the job market failed to absorb the growing number of graduates.

Economic disparities similarly marked the post-apartheid landscape. The economic policies enacted by Mandela's administration sought to redress past inequalities, but the approach was often complicated. Initially, the focus was on macroeconomic stability and attracting foreign investment. This strategy, while aimed at empowering South Africa's economy, tended to favor established corporate interests, leaving many disenfranchised communities struggling to access meaningful economic opportunities. The ANC's commitment to a market-driven economy, coupled with a lack of adequate land reform, resulted in a situation where wealth distribution remained deeply skewed.

The economic legacy of apartheid was pervasive, as black South Africans continued to face systemic barriers when trying to access employment, land ownership, and economic resources. The phenomenon of unemployment reached alarming heights, with young people bearing the brunt of this crisis. Many who had believed in the promise of a new democracy found themselves facing bleak job prospects, fueling social unrest and protests across the country. The public dissatisfaction was evident in widespread demonstrations that emerged as citizens called for better living conditions and opportunities—a stark reminder of the distance between Mandela's vision and the reality on the ground.

Mandela's decisions during this transitional period laid the groundwork for post-apartheid economic policy but also led to criticisms regarding his approach. Some activists believed that Mandela had compromised too much with the former apartheid regime, especially regarding negotiations that favored economic elites. This perception of betrayal among leftist factions within the ANC highlighted the growing rift between Mandela's vision of a reconciliatory approach and the increasingly radical aspirations of a disillusioned youth eager for change.

The implications of these social and economic challenges were not limited to immediate dissatisfaction; they also posed long-term threats to the stability of the new nation. As disconnection grew between the promises of the ANC and the lived experiences of ordinary citizens, the risk of political disillusionment became a pressing issue. Post-apartheid South Africa needed unity and cohesion, yet the struggle against persistent inequalities threatened to fragment society along economic and racial lines.

In this turbulent landscape, Mandela's role evolved. As he transitioned from the presidency to a more symbolic figure, his influence remained notable in shaping the narrative of the nation. Mandela actively championed reconciliation and nation-building, emphasizing that a peaceful and united South Africa could only emerge through collective responsibility and understanding. His belief in the potential for forgiveness and collaboration provided a contrasting vision to the frustrations simmering in many communities.

However, the complexities of Mandela's choices also resulted in a dual legacy. On one hand, he was revered for his significant contribution to the dismantling of apartheid and for steering South Africa toward democracy. Yet, on the other, he became a symbol of the challenges faced by the very society he had fought to liberate. Many lamented that the mechanisms for economic empowerment and social reforms fell short of their expectations, leading to feelings of nostalgia for a time when activism seemed more potent and hope for sweeping societal change felt more tangible.

The ongoing implications of Mandela's decisions echoed in the corridors of power long after he left office. Political leaders following Mandela had the challenge of continuing his vision while addressing the mounting pressures from constituents who demanded more than symbolic gestures of unity. The public backlash against corruption and mismanagement in subsequent years further highlighted the importance of accountability in governance. Citizens increasingly scrutinized their leaders, demanding that they deliver on commitments made in the wake of apartheid.

In contemporary South Africa, the struggle for equity and justice remains an abiding issue. Despite their tumultuous history, many South Africans embraced the ideals of the Constitution, which sought to guarantee equal rights for all. However, the realization of these ideals has repeatedly been challenged by social injustice, violence, and economic inequality. The spirit of resistance, which flourished during the anti-apartheid struggle, continues to manifest as young activists rise to demand change, often drawing inspiration from Mandela's commitment to justice and equality.

The paradox of Mandela's legacy is illustrated in this ongoing struggle for transformation. His unwavering belief in dialogue and reconciliation is deeply embedded in the fabric of the nation. Yet, it also raises critical questions about the effectiveness of such approaches in the face of systemic barriers. The balance between hope and disappointment remains delicate, as South Africa strives to navigate the complexities of its past while forging a cohesive future.

As post-apartheid South Africa continues to grapple with its legacy, Mandela's role remains vital in understanding the societal transitions at play. His leadership and vision are invoked in discussions about how to move forward, but they also serve as a reminder of the evolving nature of governance and the persistent challenges of injustice. The journey toward a fully equitable society is ongoing, shaped by the voices of those who continue to advocate for the rights of the marginalized.

Ultimately, Mandela's imprint on South Africa goes beyond the political sphere. His life and choices have become a lens through which contemporary society can examine its struggles and aspirations. The quest for justice, equality, and dignity persists, urging the nation to confront its challenges head-on while holding onto the ideals that defined its liberation movement. The legacy of a society in transition remains a work in progress, propelled by the collective commitment of a new generation willing to dream, fight, and build a better future for all.

The Threads of Reconciliation

In the aftermath of apartheid, South Africa found itself at a critical juncture. The social fabric of the nation was torn apart by decades of institutionalized racism, violence, and oppression. Healing these deep wounds required more than mere political change; it demanded a concerted effort to confront the past and foster reconciliation among a divided populace. At the heart of this endeavor was the Truth and Reconciliation Commission (TRC), an innovative yet contentious mechanism aimed at unveiling the truth behind historical injustices while promoting national healing and unity.

The establishment of the TRC was one of Nelson Mandela's pivotal decisions as South Africa transitioned from authoritarian rule to a democratic state. With his long-standing commitment to human rights and reconciliation, Mandela recognized that for democracy to flourish, it was imperative to confront the atrocities of the past openly and honestly. The TRC was thus created through the Promotion of National Unity and Reconciliation Act, passed in 1995, and it embodied a radical departure from conventional justice models that sought retribution. Instead, the TRC focused on telling the truth about past abuses while facilitating restorative justice.

Mandela's leadership throughout the formation and operation of the TRC demonstrated his remarkable vision for a new South Africa. He understood that the wounds of apartheid could not simply be swept under the rug, nor could they be resolved through punitive measures. For Mandela, healing required acknowledgment and understanding of the collective trauma experienced by both victims and perpetrators. The TRC aimed to create a space where the stories of the oppressed could be told, and where the voices of those who had committed acts of violence could be heard in a context of truth and accountability.

The commission, chaired by the respected Anglican bishop Desmond Tutu, became a symbol of hope and possibility for many South Africans. It held public hearings across the nation, offering victims of apartheid an opportunity to share their harrowing experiences and seek acknowledgment for their suffering. The testimonies revealed the extent of human rights violations, from forced disappearances and torture to systemic injustices inflicted upon entire communities. Ordinary citizens emerged as witness-bearers, recounting both the brutality they had endured and the courage they displayed during the struggle against apartheid.

Yet, the TRC was not without its criticisms and controversies. Some argued that the commission's emphasis on reconciliation came at the expense of true justice. The idea of granting amnesty to perpetrators of politically motivated crimes, as long as they were willing to tell the truth about their actions, raised profound ethical dilemmas. Victims and their families often grappled with the notion that forgiveness could lead to the erasure of accountability for those who had committed heinous acts.

Critics contended that the TRC's approach could diminish the severity of the crimes committed during apartheid and inadvertently provide a shield for human rights abuses. What, they pondered, did true reconciliation mean for the families of those who had been murdered, tortured, or disappeared? Could the nation genuinely reconcile when many felt that justice had not been served? This tension highlighted the inherent challenges of balancing the need for healing with the intrinsic desire for accountability.

Moreover, the TRC's hearings were often marked by emotional turmoil as victims recounted their trauma. The process of public storytelling, while cathartic for many, also necessitated a confrontation with painful memories that could be re-traumatizing. Witnesses often struggled to articulate their experiences, confronting not only the horror of their pasts but also the current societal dynamics that continued to evoke feelings of alienation and distrust.

Despite these challenges, Mandela remained steadfast in his belief that reconciliation was essential for the nation's future. He recognized that the TRC could serve as an educational tool, crucial for informing citizens about the nation's painful history and fostering a culture of forgiveness and understanding among disparate communities. Mandela's vision was anchored in the idea that acknowledging pain was a means to create a shared national identity — one that embraced the complexities of the past whilst paving the way for an inclusive future.

> **"Action without vision is only passing time."**
>
> — Nelson Mandela

In his public statements, Mandela continually emphasized the importance of moving forward united rather than allowing the collective trauma of apartheid to fracture the new democracy. His insistence on dialogue over confrontation echoed throughout the nation, and it provided the moral foundation upon which the TRC operated, fostering a spirit of collective healing rather than division.

However, reconciliation demanded more than acknowledgment and forgiveness; it required structural changes to address the socioeconomic disparities that apartheid had institutionalized. As part of the TRC's mandate, a series of recommendations emerged, emphasizing the need for land reform, government transparency, and the protection of human rights. Though these recommendations were noble in intent, the political reality of post-apartheid South Africa presented significant challenges. The push for healing and transformation faced resistance from various quarters, with many feeling that the TRC's focus had diverted attention from pressing social and economic issues.

The legacy of the TRC is multifaceted and complex. While it succeeded in bringing numerous stories to light, fostering a culture of discussion around forgiveness, and encouraging personal healing, the challenges it faced illustrated the difficulties of building a national identity amidst a legacy of injustice. The dichotomy between the need for accountability and the desire for reconciliation persisted long after the TRC concluded its work, shaping future discourses about the legacy of apartheid.

In the years following the TRC's closure, public sentiment towards the commission has remained a topic of heated discussion. Some view it as a success story, a groundbreaking effort to navigate one of the most fraught challenges in modern history. Others remain critical, perceiving it as a symbolic gesture that failed to adequately address the systemic inequalities that continued to plague South Africa.

Mandela's unwavering faith in the TRC and its objectives illustrated his remarkable leadership style, deeply rooted in empathy and a long-term vision for a cohesive nation. By promoting dialogue, he sought to dismantle the binaries of victim and perpetrator, calling for a reconciliation that factored in the nuances of human experience. His belief that understanding and forgiveness were crucial for healing was a fundamental tenet of his approach to leadership: a lesson he had learned through his own experiences during the struggle.

The TRC's endeavor to document the truth of apartheid's violations was one path towards collective memory, but it also laid bare the remnants of trauma that threatened to undermine national unity. As Mandela envisioned, the real challenge lay not solely in revealing the past, but in constructing a future where every South African could feel a sense of belonging, dignity, and hope. This quest for healing, though fraught with complexities, has continued to resonate in the conscious efforts of South African society to grapple with its history.

The threads of reconciliation interwoven by the TRC encompassed the voices of survivors, activists, and even those who had inflicted harm, each contributing to a broader historical narrative. The ongoing dialogues and initiatives stemming from the TRC serve to remind South Africans of their collective journey toward transformation, emphasizing that reconciliation is not a linear path but rather a multifaceted and evolving process.

Mandela's legacy in the context of the TRC, then, rests on his ability to navigate this intricate web of human experience, using his moral authority to guide the nation towards dialogue, understanding, and ultimately a more inclusive society. His commitment to reconciliation underscored the essence of leadership, demonstrating how the courage to confront one's history could yield profound transformations at both personal and national levels.

The significance of the Truth and Reconciliation Commission reverberates today, as South Africa continues to contend with the shadows of its past while striving towards a more equitable future. The discussions that emerged from the commission have prompted ongoing efforts to examine systemic injustices, engage in restorative practices, and build bridges among communities. Mandela's patient insistence on reconciliation as a vital avenue toward nation-building serves as a poignant reminder of the power of collective memory in shaping societies.

However, the journey is ongoing and the lessons learned from the TRC highlight the complexities of navigating a divided past while forging a shared future. As South Africa continues to address its layered identities and stark inequalities, the story of the TRC remains a crucial chapter in the country's ongoing narrative of healing. Mandela's vision of unity and his steadfast efforts to foster reconciliation continue to inspire and challenge future generations, urging them to grapple with the intricacies of memory, justice, and the enduring quest for national unity.

Mandela's Enduring Legacy

As South Africa moved into the 21st century, the shadows of apartheid began to disperse, giving way to a new era marked by the promise of democracy and a deeper understanding of justice. At the forefront of this change was Nelson Mandela, a figure whose legacy became intrinsically woven into the nation's fabric. His life's work was not merely confined to the struggles of his own era; rather, it laid the fundamental groundwork on which contemporary South Africa stands. This subchapter explores the profound impact of Mandela's legacy, illustrating how the principles of forgiveness, reconciliation, and leadership continue to resonate in the hearts and minds of South Africans and inspire movements for justice worldwide.

Mandela's passing in December 2013 marked not only the loss of a beloved leader but also the crystallization of a legacy that transcended national borders. Memorials, tributes, and celebrations echoed the world over, affirming Mandela's global stature as a champion of human rights. Yet, even as the tributes poured in, questions loomed about the efficacy of his ideals in a society still grappling with the complex realities of inequality and division.

In contemporary South Africa, Mandela's philosophy of forgiveness offers a poignant reminder of the power that reconciliation holds over revenge. In a nation that endured decades of brutal suppression, Mandela's call for understanding—the willingness to engage in dialogue with former oppressors—did not come easily. It required tremendous courage and vision. The Truth and Reconciliation Commission (TRC), which Mandela endorsed, became a beacon illuminating the path toward national healing. It was a radical departure from a cycle of vengeance often witnessed in post-conflict societies. The testimonies of victims and perpetrators alike served to document the nation's collective trauma, underscoring the necessity of addressing past injustices to cultivate a shared future.

Nevertheless, the effectiveness of the TRC remains a contentious topic, one that encapsulates the ongoing struggle to fully realize Mandela's vision. Critics argue that the commission failed to hold accountable many of those in power, thereby leaving deep-seated grievances unresolved. Young South Africans today, particularly those from disadvantaged backgrounds, often express skepticism about whether Mandela's ideals are genuinely upheld in a country where economic disparities are still stark. This skepticism gives rise to movements demanding justice, equity, and accountability—reminding us that the fight for social justice is ongoing and that Mandela's legacy, while powerful, is not infallible.

Mandela's leadership provides another crucial element for future generations. His ability to unite disparate groups under the banner of a shared humanity is a guiding principle for aspiring leaders. The lessons drawn from his life have been distilled into a rich narrative of hope, resilience, and commitment to collective progress. By focusing on dialogue over discord and cooperation over competition, Mandela forged a path that today's leaders can emulate. In a world that frequently witnesses the fracturing of societies along ethnic, political, and economic lines, Mandela's emphasis on collaboration, mutual respect, and understanding offers a counter-narrative that can foster unity.

This legacy is not confined to political leaders. In various sectors of South African society—including education, arts, and activism—Mandela's ideas have taken root. Educational institutions now incorporate principles of social justice into their curriculums, teaching students about the importance of empathy, civic engagement, and community service. Furthermore, countless grassroots organizations continue his work, advocating for marginalized communities and holding those in power accountable. These initiatives remind us that true leadership is not just about holding office; it is about effecting change in everyday lives.

Across Africa, Mandela's principles have inspired movements that challenge autocratic rule and demand social equity. Leaders inspired by his journey have emerged, advocating for democracy and human rights. From the streets of Cairo to the protests in Harare, Mandela's image remains a symbol of hope—an emblem of the enduring quest for justice. His influence extends into the global sphere, resonating with activists fighting against systemic injustices worldwide.

Moreover, Mandela's legacy finds expression through cultural narratives that continue to flourish. South African literature, music, and art are replete with references to his life, serving as a canvas for collective memory and reflection. Artists draw from Mandela's spirit to craft works that provoke thought and mobilize social consciousness, ensuring that the dialogue surrounding identity, belonging, and justice remains vibrant and relevant. These cultural expressions are byproducts of his enduring impact, fostering a collective sense of identity that is both diverse and inclusive.

> **"I never lose. I either win or learn."**
>
> — Nelson Mandela

Mandela's legacy also poses pertinent questions for various sectors of South African society. As the country grapples with challenges such as corruption, economic inequality, and service delivery failures, the invocation of Mandela's name acts as both an honor and a challenge.

Can today's leaders embody his spirit of selflessness, integrity, and commitment to service? Are they willing to prioritize the well-being of their constituents above personal ambition? The juxtaposition of Mandela's ethical framework against contemporary governance reveals significant disparities, prompting crucial discussions about the nature of leadership.

The younger generations, in particular, are instrumental in reinterpreting and reshaping Mandela's legacy. As South Africa confronts the legacies of apartheid that persist in economic and social disparities, youth-led movements advocate for radical change. The #FeesMustFall and #EndSARS movements exemplify this drive, as young activists take up the torch, demanding accountability and justice in ways that reflect a deep understanding of Mandela's vision for equality.

Despite the challenges South Africa faces, Mandela's legacy instills hope—an unwavering belief that change is possible. This hope permeates the very essence of South African society, from the bustling streets of Johannesburg to the rural communities of the Eastern Cape. Through grassroots campaigns, art, education, and civic engagement, the ideals Mandela championed live on, inspiring a new generation to envision a future where justice prevails.

This perspective is vital in understanding the broader implications of Mandela's legacy. As South Africans navigate the complexities of their identity and envision their future, they often turn to Mandela's principles as a compass. His story embodies the struggle against oppression but also serves as a guide for nurturing an inclusive, democratic society. The resilience of his legacy reflects the intertwining threads of history, cultural narratives, and social justice, uniting generations around the values he epitomized.

In grappling with Mandela's legacy, it becomes imperative to engage with it critically. While his ideals continue to inspire, a nuanced understanding is necessary to confront the challenges of a rapidly changing world. The aspiration for justice remains a living force that demands reflection and action. As conversations surrounding equity and justice unfold, they bring forth the complexities of embracing Mandela's legacy in a contemporary context—where his calls for forgiveness and reconciliation are often tested and challenged.

Ultimately, Mandela's legacy invites engagement, compelling South Africans—and indeed the world—to reflect on their paths toward justice. It offers a rich tapestry of narratives that inspire individuals to seek transformative change through empathy and solidarity. The principles of forgiveness and reconciliation serve as guiding stars, illuminating the path for future generations as they navigate their roles within society. While challenges abound, the spirit of Mandela continues to imbue South Africa with hope, resilience, and an unwavering commitment to social justice. Through collective memory, cultural expression, and grassroots activism, his legacy endures, ensuring that the dawn of democracy is not merely a historical event, but an ongoing journey toward an equitable future for all.

A Footprint in the Sand

> *"As we let our own light shine, we unconsciously give other people permission to do the same."*
>
> — Nelson Mandela

Public Perception Post-Presidency

Nelson Mandela's post-presidency years present a rich tapestry of public perception that encapsulates the complexity of a beloved leader transitioning from the pinnacle of political power to a celebrated elder statesman. The narratives surrounding his life after the presidency—ranging from elevated admiration to disillusionment—reflect not only individual perspectives but also the shifting landscape of South African society and global politics. This intricate interplay of perceptions, forged in the crucible of Mandela's multifaceted legacy, calls for a thorough examination to capture both the romanticized reverence and the critical appraisals that emerged in the years following his tenure as South Africa's first black president.

In the immediate aftermath of leaving office in 1999, Mandela was dutifully celebrated, revered not just as a former leader but as a symbol of triumph over adversity. His image, carefully crafted during the anti-apartheid struggle, embedded in the hearts of many South Africans and across the globe, evoked a deep sense of hope. As thousands flocked to his public appearances, Mandela was often greeted as a messianic figure, the personification of liberation, reconciliation, and national unity. Television screens and newspaper headlines showcased jubilant celebrations of his significance, turning poignant moments from his presidency into enduring fables of resilience.

> **"I am not a saint, unless you think of a saint as a sinner who keeps on trying."**
>
> — Nelson Mandela

However, this adoration also masked an evolving relationship that would unfold in the years to come. With the passage of time, revelations about the complexities of governance during his administration began to surface, painting a more intricate picture that contradicted the initially unblemished narrative. The processes of nation-building, fraught with challenges such as high unemployment, rampant crime, and discrepancies in wealth distribution, challenged the idyllic perception of Mandela's reign.

As South Africa stepped into the 21st century, Mandela became synonymous with themes of reconciliation, but this was juxtaposed against a backdrop of socio-economic issues that persisted unabated. For many South Africans, the lived reality sharply contrasted with the hopes that were ignited during the anti-apartheid struggle. Disenchantment arose not purely from unmet expectations but also from the palpable frustrations with the new leadership that took the reins after Mandela. His legacy, once untouchable, faced scrutiny and debate regarding its actual impact on the nation's trajectory.

To explore the shifting perceptions of Mandela, it is crucial to examine specific revelations that emerged in the public domain. As the years unfolded, numerous political and personal controversies circulated in the media, leading to polarized sentiments. One such revelation arose from the growing critique of his successor, Thabo Mbeki, whose policies diverged sharply from Mandela's vision of inclusivity and social justice. The discontent towards Mbeki's governance—characterized by denialism regarding the HIV/AIDS crisis, which had devastating effects on South African society—cast a shadow over Mandela's earlier efforts. Many began to reassess Mandela's legacy in light of the new challenges that felt painfully familiar; the despondency stemming from leadership's failure to prioritize critical health issues resonated deeply among those who had placed their faith in the promises of a post-apartheid era.

Furthermore, revelations about Mandela's approach to economic policy also complicated the previously uniform adulation. The neoliberal framework embraced by the government under Mbeki, which led to policy positions favoring globalization and economic liberalization, increasingly alienated Mandela's earliest supporters, who had fought against economic injustices and inequalities. Mandela's own support for these policies, as he sought to entrench stability in an economically volatile context, sparked debates regarding the efficacy of adopting a path that neglected the urgent needs of marginalized citizens. This dissonance between people's expectations and economic realities became a catalyst for reevaluation, provoking both criticism and nostalgia for a time when hope felt more tangible.

A notable phenomenon during Mandela's post-presidency was the ambivalence towards his moral authority in light of the complicity of his contemporaries in the political landscape. High-profile corruption cases and the machinations within the African National Congress (ANC) stirred deep resentment and challenged the collective memory of liberation. Some narratives framed Mandela as a reluctant leader who recognized the systemic failures that ensued, yet failed to enact potent reforms to guard against the corrosion of moral leadership within the party. For the emerging generation of activists who had grown up during Mandela's presidency, the disillusionment was overwhelmingly palpable, as they grappled with the discrepancy between their revolutionary ideals and the political realities of the ANC administration.

As South Africans ambled through the early 2000s, public opinion surrounding Mandela's legacy began to coalesce into distinct phases. In the early years, his presence epitomized peace and leadership, as demonstrated in light of his ongoing involvement in community initiatives and humanitarian projects both nationally and internationally. Notably, Mandela's efforts to combat HIV/AIDS raised awareness and hope within a society battered by the disease. His candid discussions regarding his own son's death from AIDS led to greater dialogue surrounding the epidemic, helping to destigmatize the illness and promote education.

However, this engagement prompted some to critically assess whether Mandela's philanthropic endeavors masked more significant governance issues that went unaddressed. Would it have been more powerful for him to utilize his political influence to advocate for these causes at the policy level during his presidency? This line of questioning fostered a growing recognition that the specter of unfulfilled social commitments hung over his legacy.

Contrastingly, as the world celebrated Mandela's legacy on various international platforms, a dichotomy emerged between the narrative constructed by global audiences and the lived experiences of South Africans. Internationally, he often appeared as a unifying icon emblematic of democratic leadership, meritocracy, and reconciliation. Awards, accolades, and regal receptions at foreign dignitaries' tables cemented his status in the global hierarchy of humane leadership. Yet, for many, the idea of Mandela as a saintly figure meant little when juxtaposed against the harsh realities of daily life.

These conflicted narratives were amplified through the prism of South Africa's transition toward identity formation. The struggle between holding on to his ideals while grappling with ongoing struggles regarding governance, corruption, and disillusionment forged a cultural moment that sought to remedy the fragmentation of hope. The dynamic reflection upon Mandela's life post-presidency suggested that any stable understanding of legacy must navigate through both reverence and critique.

In the years leading up to his passing in 2013, the South African context had evolved further, and Mandela found himself increasingly distanced from politics. His role shifted toward that of a symbolic figure, and he became almost a sainted relic of the anti-apartheid movement, revered yet removed from the contentious landscape of South African politics. His absence from the political scene gave way to an examination that questioned whether a 'Mandela' figure was still viable in a society confronting harsh realities.

As the world watched, the narratives that developed during his retirement reflected this growing complexity. Notably, younger generations embraced a more nuanced understanding of Mandela, one that neither venerated him solely as a flawless hero nor condemned him as a failed leader. Instead, many found themselves navigating the complexities of his life, often imbibing lessons of humility, resilience, and a relentless spirit for justice that transcended the flawed realities of leadership.

Mandela's passing triggered an outpouring of emotions, revisiting his narrative with fresh eyes. The collective mourning transformed public perception into a moment of rediscovery—a time when South Africans across the divides of age, race, and class sought to grapple with his impact. The public's reflections, much like the resonance of his life's complexities, stretched far beyond his years in office; they impacted the fabric of a nation learned from struggle and uplifted by hope.

In contrast to this outpouring of affection, however, critical appraisals surfaced anew as scholars, political analysts, and activists unpacked the layers of disappointment in leadership that persisted after his death. The complications that arose in investigating the elements of his legacy revealed an unresolved tension between the ideals he stood for and the realities that lingered. As such, Mandela's post-presidency life serves as a reminder of the dichotomies inherent in leadership; it evokes both admiration and critique, depending upon the vantage point from which one engages with history.

This evolving perception of Mandela—past and present—urges a dialogue that reflects the complexities of nation-building in post-apartheid South Africa. It is this intricate negotiation with Mandela's legacy that continues to shape the contemporary quest for justice, equality, and national identity, embodying a myriad of interpretations woven into the very fabric of society.

The perceptions surrounding Mandela's post-presidency years underscore a rich, multifaceted narrative that parallels South

Africa's continuing evolution. His life post-presidency invites a critical reassessment that acknowledges the need for accountability while still celebrating the profound contributions he made to the liberation of South Africa. The duality of these perceptions—lovingly idealized yet realistically critiqued—echoes the overarching theme of balancing hope and disappointment while striving for a more equitable future.

Revisiting Vision and Values

In the annals of history, few figures loom as large as Nelson Mandela, whose legacy continues to evoke discussions and deliberations around governance, leadership, and societal ideals. As South Africa's first black president and a symbol of resilience in the fight against apartheid, Mandela's governing principles have left a profound imprint on the nation's political landscape and the broader continent. In this dialogue, we revisit the core values that guided Mandela, examining their implications for the leaders who followed him and addressing the intersection of popular demands and political leadership in a nation still grappling with its tumultuous past.

Mandela's vision for a liberated South Africa was fundamentally rooted in principles of equality, justice, and reconciliation. Upon assuming the presidency in 1994, he sought to chart a new course for a divided nation. He understood that the path to healing was not merely a political one but a deeply emotional and psychological journey for the people of South Africa. His commitment to reconciliation over retribution illustrated a pivotal aspect of his governance—prioritizing nation-building over personal or partisan gain. By leading with empathy, Mandela instilled a culture of understanding in a society reeling from decades of systemic oppression.

Central to Mandela's governance was his belief in the power of unity. He recognized that the strength of the new nation lay not just in its diverse cultures and ethnicities but in the realization that all South Africans shared a fundamental desire for peace and prosperity. Education was a cornerstone of his administration's policies, reflecting his understanding that informed citizens are empowered citizens. Under his leadership, major strides were made in expanding access to education, with an emphasis on not only academic achievements but also on instilling values of respect and dignity among all South Africans.

However, the idealism that defined Mandela's presidency faced several challenges shortly after he left office in 1999. The intersection of popular demand and political leadership became increasingly complex as the nation moved further from the climactic moments of liberation. The euphoria that characterized the end of apartheid began to wane, with public expectations growing in tandem with rising frustrations. Citizens who had longed for change were now yearning for tangible results, eager to witness a transformation of their everyday lives into one characterized by equity and upliftment.

Post-Mandela, the ANC grappled with the daunting task of transitioning from a liberation movement into a governing entity with the responsibility of delivering on the promised ideals of his administration. Many leaders emerged from within the ranks of the ANC, yet they found themselves in a paradoxical position: the expectations placed upon them were monumental, while the realities of governance demanded compromises that often conflicted with the revolutionary ideals of the past.

For instance, Thabo Mbeki, who succeeded Mandela, emphasized economic growth and investment, proposing policies that sometimes appeared to sidestep the immediate needs of the underprivileged. The push for a market-driven economy, often criticized for overshadowing the promises of land reform and wealth redistribution, ignited debates within the party and civil society about what true liberation entailed. Activists who had once rallied behind the ideals of the ANC found themselves at odds with leaders who prioritized fiscal stability over social welfare initiatives.

The tensions surrounding these emerging policies highlighted the complex interplay between popular demand and political leadership. While the electorate desired rapid change, the realities of global economics and governance constrained the leaders' ability to deliver comprehensively on those desires. This ideological schism contributed to perceptions of complacency and disillusionment among segments of South African society. The ensuing social movements, such as the rise of the Treatment Action Campaign, illustrated how citizens began to take matters into their own hands, stressing that accountability must remain at the forefront of governance.

> **"I never cared much for personal accolades. What mattered most was the liberation of my people."**
>
> — Nelson Mandela

Mandela's legacy, while initially heralded as a beacon of hope, began to evolve into a lens through which leaders were scrutinized. The public remembered his calls for moral leadership and integrity, leading to heightened expectations for his successors. Many citizens expressed dismay at the corruption scandals and governance failures that increasingly peppered the post-apartheid political landscape. Mandela's vision of accountability and ethical leadership fueled a growing demand for transparency and responsiveness from political figures, framing the contemporary discourse around political legitimacy.

In this dialogue on governance and vision, one can observe that Mandela's commitment to negotiation as a pathway to peace became a double-edged sword. His emphasis on compromise and collaboration was instrumental in avoiding civil strife during the transition. However, this same principle, when wielded by later leaders, led to accusations of betrayal among purists who felt that the original revolutionary ideals were being sacrificed at the altar of political expediency. The subtle balance between maintaining a framework of negotiation while addressing the stark realities of inequality and poverty became a recurring theme in the discourse following Mandela's presidency.

Equally important to Mandela's vision was his belief in collective leadership. He understood the folly of centralized power and emphasized the importance of unity among various leaders within the ANC and allied movements. This principle was pivotal in ensuring that various voices were represented and heard, fostering a sense of ownership among all South Africans in rebuilding their nation. Yet, in the years following Mandela's presidency, this ethos began to erode, as factionalism and patronage politics emerged within the ANC. This shift created an environment where individual ambition sometimes overshadowed collective progress, further complicating the relationship between popular demand and political direction.

As governance evolved post-Mandela, it also became clear that the desire for transformation extended beyond mere electoral politics. Civil society emerged as a critical force, demanding accountability, highlighting social injustices, and pushing leaders to align policies more closely with the needs of the populace. Grassroots movements, including student protests and labor organization efforts, contributed to a more vibrant democracy, one that was unafraid to challenge the traditional power structures. Through these movements, citizens returned to the ideals espoused by Mandela—calling for justice, equality, and a government that works for the people.

The dialogue around Mandela's guiding principles and their implications for future leaders also unearths the challenge of aligning vision with effective governance. Leaders who succeeded Mandela often echoed his call for reconciliation and empowerment, yet their methods and outcomes frequently fell short of expectations. This disparity raised crucial questions: How do leaders uphold the moral imperatives of revolutionary ideals within the practical confines of governance? How do they cultivate a political culture that reflects Mandela's principles while being held accountable to the will of the people?

Mandela's notion of servant leadership resonates powerfully within discussions of contemporary governance. His emphasis on humility, service, and community-building formed the bedrock of his leadership style. The challenge for successors has been to embody these principles while navigating an increasingly complex political landscape. Balancing populist demands, national interests, and economic realities necessitated a recalibration of strategies that adhered to Mandela's ethical framework without losing sight of the pragmatic needs of South Africans.

As we reflect on this dialogue, it becomes clear that Mandela's vision continues to inform the aspirations of many South Africans, creating a robust narrative around leadership ideals. The values of justice, empathy, and reconciliation that he championed resonate as guiding beacons for future generations. Yet, the journey of post-apartheid governance has demonstrated that translating these ideals into effective policies requires both courage and resilience from leaders forged in a liberated society.

In conclusion, exploring Mandela's guiding principles in governance reveals both the triumphs and trials faced by a nation in transition. The complexities of aligning popular demand with political leadership underscore the challenges that come with navigating a transformed landscape. As South Africa continues to grapple with inequalities and the ambitions of its citizens, Mandela's legacy offers a steadfast reminder of the possibilities inherent in a vision grounded in hope, unity, and unwavering commitment to justice. The interplay between Mandela's ideals and the subsequent realities faced by leaders is an ongoing dialogue—a dynamic conversation that remains vital for future generations seeking to forge pathways toward equity and healing in the wake of oppression.

Enduring Influence over Generations

The legacy of Nelson Mandela is profound, transcending the boundaries of time and geography, resonating powerfully across generations. His teachings, steeped in the principles of justice, equality, and reconciliation, continue to inspire those on the frontlines of social change. In this exploration, we delve into the enduring influence of Mandela, spotlighting contemporary activists who draw motivation from his life's work. Through their voices, we see how Mandela's choices have not only shaped the political landscape of South Africa but have also woven themselves into the global tapestry of human rights movements.

To understand Mandela's impact, we begin by reflecting on the core tenets of his philosophy—principles that have become foundational to social justice advocates around the world. At the heart of Mandela's thinking was the idea of collective struggle, a philosophy rooted in the belief that the fight for justice is not merely a personal endeavor but a communal responsibility. Activists today echo this sentiment, emphasizing the necessity of solidarity in addressing systemic injustices.

Among these modern voices is Thandi Mwale, an activist working within South Africa's youth-led movements. When asked about Mandela's influence on her work, she illuminates the foundational lessons she draws from him. "Mandela taught us to fight for justice without resigning ourselves to despair. His resilience in the face of unimaginable adversity empowers me every day. I refuse to be limited by circumstances; I build coalitions and foster collective action, just as he did. We cannot forget our shared purpose—this struggle is not just about us, it's about generations to come."

Mwale's reflections echo the sentiments of many who still see Mandela as a guiding light. This sense of unity has been pivotal for contemporary movements. The calls for environmental justice, gender equality, and anti-racism are amplified through the understanding that these issues are interconnected. Mandela's fight against apartheid serves as a powerful reminder that oppression, in its myriad forms, can be dismantled through unwavering commitment to justice and collective action.

This connection to Mandela's legacy is not limited to South Africa. Across the globe, the teachings of Nelson Mandela continue to serve as a blueprint for activism in diverse contexts. In the United States, for example, movements advocating for racial equality trace their roots back to Mandela's ideologies. Activist Amira Johnson reflects on this connection: "Mandela's story has inspired so many of us in the United States. His fight was not just about ending apartheid; it was about envisioning a world where all human beings are treated with dignity and respect. You can see that in every protest, every call for justice; we invoke his spirit to remind ourselves that we are part of a larger story."

The reverberations of Mandela's messages can also be seen among rising leaders in social justice. The younger generation of activists, often referred to as the 'born-free' generation in South Africa, views Mandela's life through a lens of both admiration and critique. While they are deeply inspired by his journey from prisoner to president, they also grapple with the complexities of his decisions during and after the transition to democracy. This duality fosters a critical engagement with his legacy; they respect what he achieved while also acknowledging the ongoing social and economic disparities that persist.

Among this generation is Sipho Ntuli, an activist focused on economic justice. He reflects on the challenges faced by youth in contemporary South Africa. "Mandela envisioned a society where everyone had access to opportunities, but our reality is shaped by profound inequality. We honor his legacy by demanding more—more economic access, more meaningful engagement in politics, more opportunities for our communities to thrive. His struggle drives us toward greater accountability from those in power."

The narratives shared by activists like Mwale, Johnson, and Ntuli echo Mandela's insistence that leadership and struggle are intertwined with a moral compass. They emphasize the importance of ethical leadership and accountability in their endeavors, values instilled by Mandela's own dedication to serving the people. His life's work imbued a sense of duty among activists to not only engage in the fight for justice but to do so with integrity and compassion.

Throughout his life, Mandela championed the ideals of empathy and forgiveness, instructing his followers to seek reconciliation rather than retribution. This important lesson carries through to contemporary movements, where activists often face the challenge of addressing systemic injustices that necessitate both confrontation and compassion. In dialogues about justice today, the legacy of forgiveness remains a potent influence.

Activist Amina Rashida, who focuses on intersectional feminism, highlights this aspect of Mandela's teachings: "In our fight against patriarchy and racial injustice, we often face a choice between anger and understanding. Mandela's approach to reconciliation inspires me to seek solutions that promote healing rather than division. It's not easy, but it's a commitment to the future we are building together. We need to uplift each other, especially marginalized voices, to truly honor his legacy."

The ongoing struggles against inequality, whether tied to race, gender, or class, reveal how Mandela's legacy serves as a call to a multi-dimensional resistance. The connections drawn between disparate issues showcase a legacy of unity transcending individual battles. Within the socioeconomic landscape of modern South Africa, this interconnectedness challenges activists to embrace a holistic approach to justice—one that acknowledges historical legacies while advocating for contemporary reforms.

As various movements find their strength in Mandela's teachings, the global community is also influenced by his struggle for human rights. His life reiterates the timeless message that the fight against oppression is universal, and the lessons derived from his journey can inform movements around the world. Activists engaged in the Black Lives Matter movement, climate justice initiatives, or indigenous rights campaigns frequently reference Mandela's resilience, endurance, and vision for equality that persists beyond geographical borders.

The numerous interviews with activists across the globe highlight a collective aspiration to forge a world free from oppression. Contemporary struggles share common threads with Mandela's fight against apartheid. In each narrative, the urgency for justice shines brightly, spurred by the understanding that Mandela's sacrifices were not merely personal but collective, intended to benefit all humanity.

> **"Knowledge is the most valuable weapon in the struggle for freedom."**
>
> — Nelson Mandela

One striking feature of Mandela's legacy is its adaptability. The essence of his teachings provides a framework for addressing issues unique to different contexts. For instance, the recent climate strikes led by youth around the world demonstrate how the earlier calls for justice have evolved. Activists like Greta Thunberg remind us that the fight for a sustainable future is equally as important as the struggle against racial and social injustices. While their contexts differ, the underlying message remains rooted in the quest for fairness and dignity for all.

As we explore Mandela's influence over generations, it is apparent that his teachings have not only inspired action but have also invited deeper reflection on the very nature of justice. Decision-makers across politics and civic spaces are compelled to consider the moral implications of their actions, paralleling the intersection of activism and governance that Mandela navigated with such skill. The need for leaders who embody Mandela's principles—those who understand that true leadership is an act of service—is more pressing than ever.

In examining the evolution of Mandela's influence, we encounter another vital component: education. Mandela believed in the liberating power of knowledge, stating, "Education is the most powerful weapon which you can use to change the world." This belief underscores the importance of educational initiatives that instill Mandela's values among young people. Various organizations today focus on empowering youth through education, community engagement, and leadership development, embodying Mandela's commitment to nurturing the leaders of tomorrow.

Programs rooted in Mandela's ideals champion inclusivity and creativity, fostering a new generation equipped to tackle the complexities of the modern world. Initiatives that emphasize critical thinking and social responsibility draw upon Mandela's legacy, teaching the importance of questioning injustice and understanding history's impact on current struggles.

As we consider the influence of Mandela's teachings, it becomes clear that there exists a robust continuum that connects past, present, and future generations in an ongoing struggle for justice. Portraits of Mandela, adorned with messages of hope and resistance, continue to adorn walls not only in South Africa but across the globe in protest spaces, classrooms, and community centers. Through visual art and storytelling, his life is celebrated worldwide, reinforcing that the fight is not done and that each generation must carry the torch forward.

The stories of those inspired by Mandela offer a glimpse into the tapestry of activism that weaves through our shared humanity. Stories of resilience, triumph over adversity, and the relentless quest for dignity reflect the spirit he embodied. The activism of today is a message to the generations that will follow—an affirmation that the battle for justice is a collective responsibility, an endeavor fueled by the dreams and aspirations of many.

As we embrace the lessons of Mandela's legacy, it is essential to recognize that the journey he embarked upon was never solely about attaining power. Rather, it was about fostering change through unity, empathy, and an unwavering commitment to justice. Activists today are charged with the responsibility of evolving this legacy, continuing to weave Mandela's teachings into the fabric of their movements, ensuring that the hope he inspired does not fade away but flourishes anew with each passing generation.

Thus, while the influences of Mandela are numerous and varied, what remains most profound is the shared commitment to a collective future framed by justice, dignity, and equality. As activists navigate their paths, they carry forward the stories, hopes, and dreams that Mandela ignited. His legacy remains a compass for those seeking guidance in their quest for a better world—a world in which justice and equality reign supreme. In this enduring influence over generations, the spirit of Nelson Mandela is alive and thriving, inspiring new legacies of hope and change that will echo far beyond the sands of time.

Conversations
with the Ancestors

*"When a man has done what he
considers to be his duty to his people and
his country, he can rest in peace."*

— Nelson Mandela

Oral Histories of the Struggle

In the twilight years of the apartheid struggle, as South Africa
edged toward a future marked by hope and uncertainty, the oral
histories of those who fought for freedom emerged as vital testimonies
of perseverance, sacrifice, and resilience. This chapter endeavors
to weave together the voices of African National Congress (ANC)
leaders, comrades in struggle, and ordinary citizens, illustrating the
multifaceted experiences during one of the darkest chapters in South
African history.

These oral traditions do not merely recount historical events; they reflect the lived experiences of individuals who, through their stories, provide insight into the very fabric of resistance and the quest for liberation. From the bustling streets of Alexandra to the rural landscapes of the Eastern Cape, narratives arise that depict the vibrancy and the vicissitudes of the fight against systemic oppression.

"If you want to make peace with your enemy, you have to work with your enemy. Then he becomes your partner."

— Nelson Mandela

Among the ANC leadership, figures like Walter Sisulu and Oliver Tambo emerge as giants not just in their political roles but in their capacity to galvanize those around them. Sisulu's strategic vision and Tambo's diplomatic prowess are often celebrated in history books, yet the voices of those who walked alongside them in the trenches reveal the human dimensions of their leadership.

Let us begin with Mpho, who grew up in Soweto, an area forever etched in the collective memory of the nation. With teary eyes, Mpho recounts her first experience of apartheid brutality. "I remember the day the police came to our school, looking for 'instigators,' those who were fighting against the regime. They raided our classrooms, tearing apart our bags and shoving our teachers. As children, we sat petrified, realizing the cost of speaking freely. But even then, there was a fire in us, a desire to resist, to declare that we were more than just faceless victims."

Mpho's narrative is echoed by countless others who recount similar encounters. These shared experiences become part of a collective resistance ethos that galvanized a generation. Through their stories, one can sense the pulse of hope and indignation that propelled the movement forward, illuminating the path toward freedom.

In contrast to the young activists, the elders who lived through the height of resistance during the 1960s and 70s bring a sense of gravity and reflectiveness to the oral histories. Aunt Thandi, a revered figure in her community, remembers the apartheid government's relentless crackdown on dissent. "We were always in fear, yet we found strength in each other. We gathered in small groups, sharing our dreams of freedom and building networks of solidarity. We sang songs of resistance, which felt like armor against despair. Each note resonated with the promise of liberation, of a South Africa that embraced us all."

Her tales, rich with emotion and wisdom, reflect the role of culture as a bastion of resistance. Songs, stories, and even silence became powerful forms of defiance against the oppressive regime. It was during these communal gatherings that the spirit of unity flourished, characterized by the belief that they were fighting a just cause. Aunt Thandi recalls how they nominated one another to take up leadership roles within their communities. "We were not leaders in the conventional sense; we were mothers, fathers, brothers, and sisters, but we rose to the occasion as people united in purpose."

Across the aisle from the ANC leadership were the striking workers, pushing against the unforgiving machinery of apartheid. Sipho, a former mineworker from the Free State, narrates the grueling conditions in which they worked and the dire consequences of their strikes. "The bosses didn't care if we lived or died. We were expendable. But we organized ourselves, seeking fairness and change. We faced violence, but our resolve grew stronger. Each strike was not just for better pay but a statement: we are human beings deserving of dignity."

Sipho's accounts reinforce the notion that the struggle was not confined to the political leadership but was woven intricately into the very framework of labor and community organization. The resilient spirit of the miners and workers carried the weight of the revolution, their struggles interlinking with those of the ANC as they sought to dismantle the chains of oppression.

Yet, amidst this sea of courage and rebellion, ordinary citizens played perhaps the most crucial role. The stories told by women, in particular, exemplify bravery and resilience amidst systemic violence. Nomsa, a mother of three from the township of Soweto, shares her struggles to keep her family safe while engaging in activism. "Every day was a risk; I went to meetings while worrying about my children. On some nights, I would hear gunshots and wonder if I would see them again. But every time I stepped out, I did it for them, for their future. That hope drove me. Without hope, we had nothing."

Nomsa's narratives reveal how the family unit became the foundation of resistance. Women were often the unsung heroines, balancing their roles as caretakers while emerging as activists in the thick of the struggle. Their contributions, both at home and in the frontline, are integral to understanding the breadth of the movement—evidence that it was both a personal and collective battle.

The role of young people during the liberation struggle, particularly during the Soweto Uprising of 1976, is another poignant facet. Thabo, a high school student at the time, reflects on the moment that changed his life forever. "We gathered in our schools, our anger boiling over the injustices we faced. We were tired of being treated like dogs. It was a day of reckoning, not only for us but for the nation. We marched for our rights, and it felt as if we were empowered for the first time. It was beautiful and terrifying all at once."

Thabo's testimonies mirror a deeper societal awakening, where the youth recognized their critical role in shaping the future. Their relentless energy catalyzed significant political shifts, ushering in a wave of new ideas that challenged the status quo. As they took a stand, these young revolutionaries inspired those around them to join the cause, marking a significant turning point in the movement.

As we delve into the nuances of these oral histories, one cannot overlook the pain and trauma etched in the memories of those who lived through the turmoil. Kajal, an activist who organized protests and demonstrations, recounts her experience of losing friends to the violence inflicted by state forces. "Every name I lost was a blow, a reminder of what we were up against. But it solidified my purpose—I fought not just for my freedom but for them. I still carry their names in my heart, a constant reminder that our sacrifices should not be in vain."

The legacy of these struggles is evident in the tapestry woven from individual experiences. Each account, no matter how seemingly small, contributes to a broader narrative of defiance and hope. The stories of community gatherings, clandestine meetings, and shared sacrifices reveal how interconnected lives are essential in forging a unified front against injustice.

As we reflect on these diverse voices of the struggle, Mandela's narrative must also be interwoven. His own resilience in the face of adversity is echoed in the stories of the people he fought for. The empathy of Mandela, his ability to understand the pain of others, compels us to recognize the shared humanity that lies at the heart of resistance. His experiences resonate within the oral histories, validating the sacrifices made by the countless individuals who participated in the long fight for liberation.

Mandela once said, "I never lose. I either win or learn." This philosophy reverberates through the contributions of these storytellers, highlighting that each hardship faced during their lives added layers to their understanding of freedom and justice. They remind us of the fierce dedication around which the struggle coalesced—a dedication evident in the joyful celebration of life after repression, which marked the dawn of a new South Africa.

Oral histories capture more than just events; they embody the emotions, aspirations, and frustrations of a people united in their quest for freedom. With each account, layers of personal experience are peeled back, revealing insights into the indomitable spirit that characterized the anti-apartheid movement. Through the prism of these shared experiences, we begin to understand the complexities of a struggle that is not merely a fight against oppression but a quest for dignity, humanity, and belonging.

This collective memory is not static; it continues to evolve as new generations engage with it, shaping their understanding of justice and equality. In today's South Africa, where inequality still looms large, the memories of those who resisted serve as a guiding light for new movements and a profound reminder that the struggle for justice is ongoing.

As we conclude this chapter, we recognize the importance of preserving these oral histories for future generations. Whether recorded through interviews, storytelling, or community gatherings, these narratives carry the essence of what it means to fight for one's rights. They provide not only inspiration but also warnings—a reminder of the cost of complacency in the face of injustice.

The journey through the oral histories of the struggle reveals a mosaic of human experience, illustrating the immense capacity for resilience within a people united in their quest for dignity. Through the collective voice of the dissenters, freedom fighters, and ordinary citizens alike, we uncover profound truths about the power of hope, the necessity of remembrance, and the unyielding spirit of those who dared to dream of a better tomorrow.

The Collective Memory

In the wake of monumental events, the stories we choose to tell ourselves become the bedrock upon which our national identity is built. For South Africa, a country forged through struggle, resilience, and immense sacrifice, collective memory plays a crucial role in shaping how history is remembered and how futures are envisioned. From the inception of the African National Congress (ANC) to the dawn of democracy, the narratives that surround figures like Nelson Mandela have evolved, reflecting both the complexities of the nation's past and the aspirations of its people.

> **"Real leaders must be ready to sacrifice all for the freedom of their people."**
>
> — Nelson Mandela

Collective memory, as a sociological concept, refers to the shared pool of knowledge and information in the memories of members of a social group. It differs from individual memory in that it is shaped by social influences and becomes a communal narrative that can shift over time. In South Africa, this collective memory has been profoundly influenced by apartheid, a regime that sought to break down the very fabric of communal identity through systematic oppression and dehumanization. The struggle against this injustice galvanized a diverse array of voices, leading to a shared history of resistance that unites South Africans, albeit in varied and sometimes conflicting ways.

Nelson Mandela stands as a pivotal figure within this framework of collective memory. His image is not simply a construction of one narrative but rather a compilation of stories told from different perspectives that illuminate his multifaceted character. As a leader, he embodies hope, resilience, and the relentless pursuit of justice. Yet, the manner in which these attributes are emphasized varies widely, often influenced by the storyteller's own political and ideological leanings.

In post-apartheid South Africa, Mandela's image was initially enveloped in a romanticized aura, celebrated as the ultimate hero who triumphed over tyranny. This glorification served to unify a fractured society and inspire a collective spirit of reconciliation. The Truth and Reconciliation Commission (TRC), established under Mandela's leadership, epitomized this phase of collective memory. It positioned the process of forgiveness and healing at the forefront, with Mandela as its symbolic leader. The stories shared during the TRC hearings fostered a sense of shared accountability and victimhood, reframing the national narrative towards one of unity.

However, the idealization of Mandela has faced scrutiny over the years, leading to a growing discourse around historical revisionism. Scholars and activists alike have raised concerns that such glorification simplifies the complexities of his leadership and minimizes the struggles endured by various factions of the ANC and broader liberation movements. As the nation grapples with economic disparities and persistent social inequalities, the narrative of Mandela as a flawless leader is challenged by critiques that highlight the compromises he made during the transition to democracy.

Critics argue that the Mandela legacy, as constructed by mainstream narratives, risks overshadowing the contributions of women, youth, and other marginalized voices in the anti-apartheid struggle. Figures like Winnie Mandela and the youth leaders of the ANC Youth League played critical roles in advancing the struggle for liberation, but their stories remain on the periphery. This selective remembrance often discredits the ongoing struggles faced by those who do not resonate with the dominant Mandela narrative, thereby fracturing the society's collective memory by excluding significant portions of its history.

As we delve deeper into the dynamics of collective memory, it becomes essential to examine how various groups within South Africa's diverse population engage with the memory of Mandela. Indigenous cultures, diaspora communities, and urban youth infuse their unique experiences with Mandela's ideals, whether through oral traditions, literature, or new media. These engagements often highlight the contradictions in Mandela's legacy and the diverse interpretations that coalesce around his figure.

Oral history, for example, serves as a powerful medium for revitalizing the voices of those who participated in the struggle but are not represented in mainstream narratives. As stories are passed down through generations, they reflect localized understandings of the anti-apartheid struggle that enrich the national tapestry of collective memory. Each retelling adds layers to Mandela's legacy, intricately interweaving personal experiences with broader historical contexts.

Moreover, the rise of social media and digital storytelling has allowed for a democratization of memory, offering platforms for voices that have historically been silenced. Young South Africans draw upon Mandela's legacy to address contemporary issues, such as economic inequality, systemic racism, and environmental degradation. They challenge the prevailing narratives of the past, infusing them with modern-day critiques. This dynamic interplay between past and present creates a living memory that remains relevant and rooted in ongoing struggles for justice.

The debate surrounding Mandela's legacy and its implications for collective memory is further complicated by the political landscape. Political factions, including those within the ANC, have taken distinct approaches to harness Mandela's image for their own purposes. Where some scholar-activists argue for a nuanced understanding of Mandela as a leader of compromise, others view him as a martyr who sacrificed vital principles on the altar of stability. This dichotomy reveals how collective memory can be both a unifying force and a site of contention, reflecting deeper societal divisions.

Furthermore, public commemorations and monuments dedicated to Mandela reflect how societies curate their collective memory. Statues, named institutions, and memorial services serve as tangible acts of remembrance, shaping public perceptions and reinforcing narratives. Yet, these commemorative acts are not without contention. Debates about the appropriateness of certain monuments or the interpretations of Mandela's visions highlight the tensions inherent in collective memory, as individuals and groups grapple with what it means to honor a leader whose life and legacy are subject to diverging interpretations.

The ongoing conversation about collective memory in South Africa necessitates a critical engagement with the past, prompting exploration into how current realities are influenced by historical narratives. Programs that incorporate discussions around memory, history, and identity in South African curricula reflect efforts toward healing and understanding, aiming to foster a generation that is not only aware of its past but also engaged with its implications for the future. Through educational initiatives, the nuances of Mandela's life can be examined, encouraging critical thinking and prompting deeper reflections on what leadership, governance, and activism entail.

In grappling with the complexities of collective memory, it is important to recognize that the past is not static. Collective memory serves as a site of negotiation, wherein stories are reclaimed, reinterpreted, and retold in ways that resonate with new generations. As South Africa continues to navigate the winding paths of its socio-political landscape, the stories surrounding figures like Mandela will likely evolve further, influenced by contemporary contexts and the lived experiences of all citizens.

Ultimately, the essence of collective memory lies not only in the stories told but in the intent behind them. The challenge remains to embrace the entirety of the narrative—the triumphs and failures, the celebrated and the overlooked. In doing so, South Africa can cultivate a collective memory that honors the complexity and richness of its diverse heritage. This process fosters not only a deeper understanding of Nelson Mandela's role and contributions but also a commitment to inclusivity and reconciliation, nurturing a society that understands that its future is built upon the collective acknowledgment of its diverse past.

Intergenerational Storytelling

In the rich tapestry of South African history, storytelling has served as both a vessel for remembrance and a beacon of hope, particularly in the context of the anti-apartheid struggle and the legacy of Nelson Mandela. As we delve into the concept of intergenerational storytelling, it is crucial to understand how this practice not only preserves the narrative of struggle and triumph but also inspires contemporary generations to engage actively with the ideals that Mandela championed.

The very act of recounting stories has potent significance in traditional African cultures, where oral history serves as a means of passing down values, lessons, and experiences. In many South African communities, elders bear the responsibility of transmitting knowledge and wisdom to younger generations. This oral tradition fosters a sense of identity and belonging, creating a bridge that connects the past with the present and the future. Through storytelling, the narratives surrounding Mandela's life—the struggles he faced, the sacrifices he made, and the dreams he held for a unified South Africa—have trickled down through the ages, embedding a powerful legacy of resilience and hope.

> **"There is no easy walk to freedom anywhere."**
>
> — Nelson Mandela

Contemporary South Africans engage with Mandela's legacy through various platforms, some of which are traditional, while others are highly innovative. These platforms range from community gatherings, school curricula, and art forms such as theater and music to social media campaigns that celebrate his life and ideals. Each medium serves to revitalize Mandela's story, adapt it to current circumstances, and inspire new generations to continue the journey toward justice and equality.

In community gatherings, elders recount tales of Mandela's courage and unwavering commitment to freedom, emphasizing the importance of perseverance in the face of adversity. These gatherings are not merely nostalgic; they serve as call-to-action moments, reminding young people of their responsibility to carry forward the legacy of those who fought before them. In these spaces, storytelling transforms from mere retelling of events into a rallying cry for justice and involvement in present-day issues.

Schools have also become vital arenas for intergenerational storytelling, ensuring that Mandela's legacy is integrated into the formation of young minds. Curriculum developers have increasingly recognized the importance of including stories of struggle and triumph in South African history lessons, where students learn not only about Mandela's life but also about the broader collective resistance against apartheid. This educational narrative cultivates empathy and understanding, providing students with the tools to reflect critically on social injustices that persist in today's society. By weaving Mandela's journey into the school curriculum, educators are effectively instilling a sense of responsibility among the youth to honor his memory through active citizenship.

Artistic expression stands as another significant medium through which intergenerational storytelling flourishes. In contemporary South Africa, the arts—whether through theater, dance, or visual art—allow for explorations of Mandela's impact from diverse cultural perspectives. For instance, performances that depict key moments from Mandela's life can evoke powerful emotions, resonate with historical consciousness, and ignite aspirations for a more equitable society. Artists often collaborate with community members, blending traditional African storytelling techniques with modern narratives, creating dynamic representations that appeal to younger audiences.

In recent years, social media has emerged as a formative tool for storytelling among the youth. Hashtags dedicated to Mandela's memory circulate across platforms like Twitter and Instagram, empowering younger generations to claim their narratives and connect with a global audience. Young people share their interpretations of Mandela's teachings, how they influence their lives, and their aspirations for a better South Africa. This form of engagement not only democratizes the process of storytelling but also encourages communal reflection and activism, galvanizing collective efforts towards social change. When contemporary South Africans utilize digital platforms, they merge historical legacy with modernity, fostering a sense of unity and purpose.

Intergenerational conversations infuse stories with different layers of meaning, where younger generations may respond to Mandela's legacy differently than their predecessors. For many young South Africans, Mandela's ideals of forgiveness and reconciliation are juxtaposed with their lived experiences of socio-economic disparities and ongoing discrimination. This nuanced understanding fosters a critical perspective toward Mandela's vision and invites discussions on how to adapt his principles to address contemporary challenges.

Listening to the narratives of older generations, young people gain insight into the sacrifices made during the apartheid years and the ideals that motivated the struggle for liberation. This respect for the past not only generates gratitude but also inspires a commitment to advocacy rooted in the collective history of their forebears. As they examine the impact of apartheid on their lives today, the narratives of struggle ignite a passion for social justice, driving them to engage in activism that reflects the aspirations of a new generation.

Community leaders and activists acknowledge the significance of intergenerational storytelling in mobilizing young people today. They host workshops and events that celebrate the narratives of struggle while also exploring the pathways to progress. These efforts create inclusive spaces for discussion and foster a sense of agency among the youth, connecting their personal battles with the broader fight for justice. The awareness raised through these initiatives not only honors Mandela's legacy but also reaffirms the importance of each individual's role in shaping the future.

Moreover, the themes woven into these stories adapt to the contemporary landscape. Stories of unity, resilience, and hope echo through discussions about gender equality, environmental justice, and economic empowerment. Young activists invoke Mandela's spirit in their campaigns for change, drawing parallels between past and present struggles. This intertextual engagement highlights the enduring relevance of Mandela's life and work, as the global narrative around justice, peace, and human rights transcends time and geography.

As young South Africans explore Mandela's legacy in the context of their reality, they begin to articulate their vision for a better tomorrow. Equipped with the collective history and stories shared by their elders, they confront the socio-political challenges of today with renewed vigor and determination. In this way, intergenerational storytelling not only preserves the past but serves as a roadmap for future activism, where Mandela's vision for equality continues to guide their aspirations.

Encouraging young people to contribute their own narratives fosters a sense of ownership over their stories. Activism today often emphasizes personal experience and testimony, allowing individuals to share their own struggles and triumphs within the framework of Mandela's legacy. These voices form a complex mosaic, amplifying the ideas of resilience and hope while honoring the historical fighters who paved the way.

As we consider the transformative power of intergenerational storytelling, it becomes clear that it is more than mere recollection; it is a profound vehicle for empowerment. The stories passed down offer blueprints for future action, equipping young activists with the tools they need to navigate the complexities of their current struggles. These stories become a source of inspiration, reminding them that the fight for justice is ongoing and that their contributions are an integral part of the narrative.

Finally, the act of storytelling is intrinsically tied to identity, particularly in a country as diverse as South Africa. By embracing the narratives of their predecessors, young South Africans forge a connection to their roots that fosters pride in their heritage. This pride encourages a collective responsibility to honor the values of the past while actively engaging with the issues of the present. Storytelling becomes a sacred trust, a promise to remember, reflect, and act in the spirit of those who came before.

In conclusion, intergenerational storytelling exemplifies the vital transmission of hope and resilience across generations. Mandela's legacy lives on through the stories shared within families, communities, schools, and creative spaces. As contemporary South Africans continue to engage with these narratives, they not only pay homage to a remarkable leader but also construct a future grounded in the same ideals of justice, equality, and perseverance that inspired Mandela himself. Through the rich tradition of storytelling, the spirit of the struggle for liberation remains alive, guiding new generations in their pursuits for a more just and equitable society.

The Duality
of Hope

"*May your choices reflect your
hopes, not your fears.*"

– Nelson Mandela

Revolutionary Hope in Times of Despair

In examining the concept of revolutionary hope, we confront the duality that it presents within the tumultuous realm of activism and governance. Hope, as a fundamental human aspiration, acts as both a beacon guiding the oppressed through the storm of despair and a stringent taskmaster, reminding revolutionary leaders of the aspirations they have kindled. Striking a balance between idealism and the sobering realities that may accompany political change becomes an arduous endeavor. The journey towards liberation, while enshrined in lofty ideals, often collides with the gritty, unvarnished truths of governance.

In the case of Nelson Mandela and the broader struggle against apartheid, hope was not merely an abstract notion; it was a vital force that propelled the movement forward, even in the darkest hours. Mandela's own life can be viewed as a microcosm of this duality. His early years were steeped in a vision of a liberated South Africa, yet the harsh landscape of apartheid loomed heavy, presenting challenges that required pragmatic solutions rather than idealistic dreams. Thus, the nature of hope became intertwined with the realities of struggle and governance in profound and often contradictory ways.

> **"Resentment is like drinking poison and then hoping it will kill your enemies."**
>
> — Nelson Mandela

Revolutionary hope thrives in the chasms of despair, which can lead to both invigorating breakthroughs and debilitating disillusionment. Mandela's steadfastness in the face of adversity exemplifies how hope can flourish amidst the struggle, yet it also reflects the intricate tapestry of emotions that accompanies the quest for justice. As he transitioned from the confines of Robben Island to the presidency, he was confronted with the daunting reality that liberation does not equate to an end point but rather lays the groundwork for an even bigger challenge: the consolidation of a nation.

One critical aspect of understanding hope in the context of revolution is recognizing its psychological impact on both individuals and communities. Throughout the struggle against apartheid, hope served as a psychological anchor, offering resilience to those who were otherwise marginalized and oppressed. It was a thread woven through the lives of countless activists who dared to envision a future defined by democracy and equality. However, this very hope also carried the weight of expectation, placing immense pressure on leaders like Mandela to deliver tangible results. The fine line between hope and expectation can evoke powerful sentiments among the populace, generating both fervent support and simmering dissent.

In many instances, the initial excitement and energy that accompany revolutionary change can lead to disillusionment when the anticipated transformations do not materialize. For instance, Mandela entered the presidency with great fanfare, heralded by allies globally as a figure of reconciliation and change. However, beneath the surface lay significant socioeconomic disparities, unresolved issues from the past, and a population longing for swift improvements. As governance unfolded, the chasm between the aspirations ignited during the liberation struggle and the political realities of a newly formed democracy became pronounced. This duality of hope became critical in shaping the trajectory of the nation. While Mandela embodied hope during his struggle, he also faced the subsequent reality of managing expectations and navigating the complexities of power.

Critics of Mandela, particularly from within the ANC and broader sectors of society, began to voice their dissatisfaction as the relationship between revolutionary hope and achievable realities became more pronounced. The desires for radical economic transformation, social justice, and a comprehensive redress of past grievances collided with the realities of running a government that needed to negotiate and stabilize a fragile post-apartheid context. This intersection of hopes and realities serves as a poignant reminder of how easily the flame of revolutionary hope can morph into a source of tension.

Furthermore, the nuances of governance rendered it increasingly complicated for Mandela and his contemporaries to fulfill the sweeping promises articulated during the struggle. While the ideals of the Freedom Charter resonated powerfully within the liberation movement, the practical implications of implementing such ideals in governance proved more challenging than anticipated. The economic constraints, the complexity of land reform, and the disparities in service delivery illuminated the challenges of translating revolutionary optimism into mechanisms of power.

In grappling with such contradictions, one must delve into the essence of transformative leadership: the ability to balance idealism with practicality. Revolutionary hope, when interspersed with pragmatism, can harness collective energy while guiding a nation towards reasonable progress. Mandela's leadership is illustrative of this dynamic. His vision of a reconciliatory South Africa, while rooted in hope, necessitated careful negotiation with entrenched interests, as well as addressing the urgent needs of a diverse population. His approach sought to cultivate hope in a manner that embraced all voices—an ideal ingrained in the democratic values he aspired to embody.

However, the tension between hope and reality often resulted in factionalism within the ANC itself, exposing fractures that mirrored broader societal divisions. As poverty persisted and inequality became more pronounced, diverse voices emerged from the left advocating for more radical shifts, jostling against the ANC's moderating stance under Mandela's leadership. This internal schism unveiled the complexities of governance: while certain factions continued to uphold revolutionary hope as an absolute ideal, others became increasingly disillusioned, advocating for a more urgent, reformist approach to address pressing social issues.

The narrative of hope also interlinks with the collective memory of the struggle, where the reverence for Mandela as a symbol of hope juxtaposed against the critique of the ANC's governance trajectory generates a complex discourse. The struggle for liberation, taken together with the realities of post-revolutionary governance, often instigates a potent dialectic that forces societies to confront their narratives of hope and accountability. How does one navigate the tension between ideals and what is achievable? This query reverberates throughout the lives of revolutionary leaders, who are often forced to make compromises that challenge the purity of their ideals in favor of a collective stability.

The implications of hope on collective identity also highlight how nations enshrine their revolutionary struggles within a broader socio-political framework. The communal understandings of what liberation means for a thriving society often vary significantly based on historical experiences. In South Africa, the aspiration for hope created a rich palette of narratives and articulations surrounding reconciliation, economic justice, and cultural renaissance. Within this fertile ground, the community became emboldened to both celebrate accomplishments and express frustrations regarding unmet desires.

While Mandela championed unity, he also recognized the necessity of addressing the plight of the most marginalized communities. This understanding became crucial as disillusionment began bubbling within the ranks of those who fought tirelessly for societal change. While hope was essential in drawing individuals together during the struggle against apartheid, it had to withstand the complexities of addressing diverse expectations in a post-apartheid landscape. Mandela, conscious of this duality, often spoke about the importance of galvanizing hope as a continual process—one that requires vigilance against complacency and the need for gradual yet unwavering progress.

"Quitting is leading too."

— Nelson Mandela

In reflecting upon the legacy of hope, it becomes vital to consider how hope can serve as both a source of empowerment and a foundation upon which frustrations may fester. As the revolutionary fervor ebbs and flows into the realm of governance, it necessitates an analysis of what magic can still be harnessed from the revolutionary aspiration that fueled activists like Mandela. Indeed, visionary leadership grapples with the ever-present challenge: how do we sustain hope within systems that might inherently challenge our principles? This intricate dance between hope and reality will continue to shape the paths of revolutionary leaders well into the future.

Mandela's insistence on restorative justice through reconciliation, rather than retribution, exemplifies a broader understanding of how revolutionary hope must intertwine with an appreciation for shared humanity. He sought not merely to dismantle oppression but to build bridges capable of withstanding the tremors of history and the fallout from unabated societal strife. In his eyes, hope had to transform into actionable diplomacy, integrating cultural understanding within a framework that accounts for every individual's story within the larger narrative of post-apartheid South Africa.

Furthermore, understanding hope within the lens of revolutionary movements invokes a definition tied to endurance and resilience.

Thus, revolutionary hope evolves concurrently with societal transformations—sometimes faltering and reforming with external realities yet always undergirded by the desire for a better future. The journey from struggle to governance represents a transformation that constantly encounters the frictional dynamics between expectations and feasibility.

To encapsulate hope as a double-edged sword, one must acknowledge the possibility of its misuse, as it can evoke both profound agency and despair. The act of inspiring hope, while fundamentally aimed at uplifting communities, can incite disappointment when juxtaposed with unfulfilled promises. Mandela's life invites continual reflection on the ways each individual must play a role in shaping their governance by holding those in power accountable. The insatiable hunger for justice can ignite powerful movements that both inspire and challenge leadership. The narratives that emerge from these movements become essential to analyze the constructs surrounding collective memory and the ongoing struggle for justice and equity.

As a global community engaging with legacy and memory from leaders like Mandela, we are prompted to reckon with the revolutionary hopes that remain simmering beneath the surface. Those hopes are often countered by systemic realities that impede progress, creating an intricate tapestry of what liberation and governance represent in contemporary society. Embracing the essence of hope—even when it feels simultaneously burdensome and uplifting—is part of nurturing our commons, enabling us to weave the intentions of past leaders into actionable frameworks for transformative change. The continual pursuit of freedom demands that we grapple deeply with our principles, integrating hope into the very fabric of our dreams while facing the complex horizons of possibility.

Ultimately, in the exploration of revolutionary hope, we find ourselves at the intersection between memory, action, and accountability. As we navigate the narratives steeped in Mandela's legacy and others like him, we encounter the intricate nuances of what it means to be truly liberated. Post-revolutionary societies must grapple with accountability in ways that encourage both reflection and action. The deliberate act of perpetuating hope in its many forms will remain critical in the arc of progress and ensure it enriches our lands, communities, and shared stories for generations to come.

Lessons from Mandela's Journey

In examining the life and journey of Nelson Mandela, one cannot help but confront the intricacies of leadership amidst profound societal upheaval. Mandela's path offers a kaleidoscope of lessons not only for current and future leaders but also for individuals seeking to impact their communities and the world at large. His journey, interwoven with the struggles against apartheid, encapsulates the duality of hope—both the extraordinary optimism for a better future and the stark realities of the path leading to it.

As we delve into Mandela's experiences, we unearth actionable insights that resonate on personal and political levels. They compel us to reflect on our responsibilities, challenging our preconceptions of leadership and the pivotal role each of us plays in driving societal change.

One of the foremost lessons from Mandela's journey is the importance of resilience. Mandela spent 27 years imprisoned, yet he emerged not only alive but also with an unwavering commitment to peace and reconciliation. He understood that resilience is not merely the capacity to withstand hardship but also the ability to maintain one's values and vision in the face of adversity. How often do we find ourselves questioning our commitment when faced with challenges? Mandela's story urges us to cultivate resilience within ourselves, to persevere for the causes we believe in, and to be unwavering in our convictions, even when the road is fraught with obstacles.

Mandela's capacity for empathy is another profound lesson. He chose to understand the perspectives of his adversaries rather than simply vilifying them. Upon his release, rather than seeking retribution against those who had oppressed him and his people, he extended a hand of forgiveness and aimed for national healing. This shift from animosity to understanding highlights the importance of empathy in leadership. Are we, in our own spheres of influence, willing to listen to and learn from those with whom we disagree? How might our relationships and efforts toward social change flourish if we approached them with a mindset of empathy?

Moreover, one cannot overlook the significance of collaboration and inclusivity demonstrated by Mandela throughout his life. He recognized that no meaningful change could occur in isolation; it requires the voices and efforts of many. By fostering a culture of inclusivity, Mandela was able to unite a fractured nation. Whether it was through the formation of the ANC or the various coalitions he nurtured during negotiations, Mandela's achievements were rooted in collective effort. How can we, in our own communities, advocate for collaboration? Are we building alliances that embrace diverse perspectives, or are we confining ourselves within echo chambers?

Another vital lesson lies in the pursuit of education as a catalyst for change. Mandela famously stated, "Education is the most powerful weapon which you can use to change the world." His own commitment to learning and intellectual growth was evident through his voracious reading during his imprisonment. Education empowers individuals by expanding their potential and sharpening their critical thinking. Are we investing in our own education and that of others? Do we recognize the transformative power of knowledge in fueling activism and social justice?

Furthermore, Mandela's journey underscores the necessity of strategic pragmatism. While his idealism drove the vision for a free South Africa, his experiences taught him the importance of practical strategies to achieve these dreams. The negotiations that ultimately led to South Africa's transition from apartheid required significant compromises, demonstrating that effective leadership often involves balancing ideals with realistic solutions. How frequently do we criticize compromise without recognizing its strategic necessity? Are we prepared to rethink our rigid stances in favor of collaborative progress?

Mandela's adeptness in communication is another key takeaway. He possessed the remarkable ability to articulate his vision clearly and passionately, which inspired millions and galvanized movements for change. His speeches transcended mere rhetoric; they encapsulated the shared hopes and challenges of his people. How skilled are we in communicating our own visions? Do we harness the power of language to inspire action and foster unity or to further divide?

The ability to adapt is essential in leadership, as demonstrated throughout Mandela's life. From his evolution as a young radical to a seasoned statesman, he exemplified the importance of being responsive to changing circumstances. Whether in the context of negotiations or the shifting landscape of political power, Mandela's adaptability enabled him to navigate complex situations effectively. Are we remaining flexible in our approaches to leadership and social change? How can we embrace change while staying true to our core values?

Another essential insight from Mandela's life is the necessity of compassion intertwined with strength. While Mandela was a staunch advocate for justice, he never wavered in his commitment to the dignity of all individuals, including his former adversaries. This balance of compassion and resolve is critical for anyone seeking to foster change. How often do we equate strength with aggression or inflexibility? Can we redefine strength as the courage to uphold our values while being fair and humane?

> "A child is the most beautiful gift this world has to give."
>
> — Nelson Mandela

Moreover, Mandela's ability to inspire hope reminds us that leadership is as much about fostering optimism as it is about driving pragmatic outcomes. The hope Mandela instilled in his people was a powerful force that fueled the movement for equality. His capacity to envision a better future, even during the bleakest moments, galvanized others to dream and fight alongside him. In what manner do we create and sustain hope within our communities? How can we channel our personal experiences, positive or negative, to inspire and uplift others?

Lastly, it is essential to recognize that Mandela's journey teaches us that every individual has the power to effect change, regardless of their circumstances. His life is a testament to the impact of singular actions, which, when multiplied across a collective, can lead to monumental transformations. Are we acknowledging our own potential to enact change? How do our day-to-day actions contribute to the broader movement for justice?

As we reflect on these lessons distilled from Mandela's journey, we must challenge ourselves to thoughtfully assess our roles in fostering hope, resilience, empathy, and inclusivity in our communities and spheres of influence. Leadership is not confined to those in positions of power; it is a commitment that each of us can embody in our actions, attitudes, and choices.

In a world grappling with persistent inequality, social injustices, and political unrest, Mandela's legacy serves as both an inspiration and a challenge. His life exemplifies the duality of hope: the potential for radical change anchored in the realities of compromise and collaboration. As we navigate our own paths toward creating a more just society, let us strive to harness the lessons from Mandela's journey, transforming them into actionable steps that inspire we and those around us.

How are we leveraging our personal experiences and challenges as vehicles for change? What practical steps can we take today that embody the values Mandela upheld? It is essential that we engage in this introspection and strive to embody those principles of resilience, empathy, collaboration, education, pragmatic idealism, effective communication, adaptability, compassion, hope, and personal agency that Mandela so vividly exemplified.

Ultimately, as we conclude this exploration of lessons from Nelson Mandela's life, let us take these reflections and convert them into a tangible commitment for change. By understanding the complexities of leadership and the nuances involved in the pursuit of justice, we can emerge not only as passive observers but as active participants in the ongoing struggle for a better world. How can we contribute to this legacy of hope? Together, through our collective efforts and individual actions, we can honor Mandela's contributions and continue to nurture the spirit of resilience and hope that he instilled in so many.

"Lead from the back — and let others believe they are in front."

– Nelson Mandela

Thank You, Fellow Travelers!

Wow, what a journey we've had together! Thank you from the bottom of my heart for sticking with me through this wild ride. I searched high and low, crafted characters with quirks you can relate to, and wove adventures that sparked your imagination. It means the world to me that you chose to accompany me on this adventure!

As you close this book, feel that little tingle of excitement? That's the universe whispering its secrets to you, urging you on to the next grand adventure awaiting just outside the pages. I hope this tale sparked a fire in your belly, something that inspires you to leap into your own pursuits with courage and vigor!

But this isn't just a goodbye; it's a heartfelt invitation to keep the conversation going! Share your thoughts, your feelings, and your dreams with me—I'm here, and I want to know how this journey has touched your life. Let's connect and explore what's next together because the magic doesn't stop here!

Remember, every story has an end, but it also holds the potential for new beginnings. You've read about my characters, but now it's your turn to become the hero of your own story. Take the courage you found between these pages and let it propel you forward. Your adventures are waiting, just around the corner!

Lastly, let's promise to meet again someday, whether through the pages of another book or in the cosmos where our imaginations collide. As you step back into the world, know that my words are always here with you, trailblazing paths to countless adventures yet to come.

With boundless gratitude,

SOUL DIA

www.ingramcontent.com/pod-product-compliance
Lightning Source LLC
Chambersburg PA
CBHW032057020426
42335CB00011B/385